Political Choices and Electoral Consequences

Political Choices and Electoral Consequences
A Study of Organized Labour and the New Democratic Party

KEITH ARCHER

McGill-Queen's University Press
Montreal & Kingston • London • Buffalo

© McGill-Queen's University Press 1990
ISBN 0-7735-0744-2

Legal deposit third quarter 1990
Bibliothèque nationale du Québec

∞

Printed in Canada on acid-free paper

This book has been published with the help of a grant from the Social Science Federation of Canada, using funds provided by the Social Sciences and Humanities Research Council of Canada.

Canadian Cataloguing in Publication Data

Archer, Keith, 1955–
Political choices and electoral consequences
Includes bibliographical references.
ISBN 0-7735-0744-2
1. New Democratic Party. 2. Trade-unions — Canada — Political activity. I. Title.
HD6527.A73 1990   324.27107
C90-090126-8

This book was typeset 10/12 Palatino by
Typo Litho composition inc.

For Lisa

Contents

Tables/Figure   ix

Acknowledgments   xi

CHAPTER ONE
The Weakness of the NDP in Federal Politics   3

CHAPTER TWO
Choosing the Rules of Union-Party Affiliation:
A Historical Perspective   7

CHAPTER THREE
Measuring the Union Link to the NDP   27

CHAPTER FOUR
Union-Party Affiliation as a Collective Action Problem   41

CHAPTER FIVE
Electoral Consequences of Union Affiliation   56

CHAPTER SIX
Explaining Voting Behaviour in Canada   72

Notes   93

Bibliography   103

Index   111

Tables/Figure

TABLES

1 Percentage Vote for the Liberal and Conservative Parties, 1878–1984   10

2 New Democratic Party Revenue, 1979–86   34

3 Unions Affiliated with the NDP and Membership of Affiliated Unions as a Percentage of Total Union Membership, Selected Years   37

4 Organizations Affiliated to the NDP, by Province, April 1985   38

5 Number of Unions and Membership, by Type of Union in Canada, 1966 and 1984   43

6 British Trade Unions Affiliated with the TUC, by Size of Union, 1976   47

7 TUC Unions Affiliated with the British Labour Party, by Size of Union, 1976   48

8 Representation at Labour Party Conference, 1976   50

9 Canadian Unions Affiliated with the CLC, by Type of Union, 1984   51

10 CLC Unions Affiliated with the NDP, by Type of Union, 1984   53

11 Representation at NDP Convention, 1981   54

12 Party Identification and Vote, by Union Status, 1979   62

13 Party Identification and Vote, by Union Status, 1984   63

14 Party Identification and Vote, by Union Status, UAW-USWA vs. Non–UAW-USWA, 1979   65

15 Percentage NDP Identification and Vote, by Union Status, Controlling for Region and Level of Constituency Support for the NDP   67

16 NDP Leader, Party, and Candidate Thermometer Scores, by Union Status, 1979   68

17 Social Class Awareness and Class Self-Placement, by Union Status, 1979   69

18 Left-Right Subjective Class Self-Placement, by Union Status, 1979   70

19 Reciprocal Model of Liberal Vote, 1979   82

20 Reciprocal Model of Conservative Vote, 1979   85

21 Reciprocal Model of NDP Vote, 1979   87

FIGURE

1 Reciprocal Model of the Determinants of Voting   74

Acknowledgments

This book is based on a doctoral dissertation completed at Duke University. At Duke I benefited from the generous financial assistance of the Canadian Studies Center, the Graduate School, and the Department of Political Science as well as the Social Sciences and Humanities Research Council of Canada. I received much helpful advice and direction from my adviser, Allan Kornberg, and from other members of the committee, especially Peter Lange and Jack Hoadley.

At Calgary I received additional financial support from the University Research Grants Committee and clerical assistance from Ella Wensel and Judi Powell. Useful comments on various parts of the manuscript have been provided by John Bauer, David Elkins, Tom Flanagan, Jane Jenson, Lawrence LeDuc, Hudson Meadwell, Neil Nevitte, Les Pal, Tony Solari, and Alan Whitehorn, none of whom shares responsibility for what I have written. The federal office of the New Democratic party provided generous access to confidential files, for which I am grateful. An earlier version of chapter 4 appeared in *Labour/Le Travail* and previous versions of chapters 5 and 6 were published in the *Canadian Journal of Political Science*. Peter Goheen has been an especially pleasant yet persistent editor at McGill-Queen's and provided encouragement at critical points. Marion Magee has been a very helpful copy editor. My greatest debt is to my wife, Lisa, and to our children, Justin, Caitlin, Ben, Will, and Isaiah for helping to keep the project in perspective.

Political Choices and Electoral Consequences

CHAPTER ONE

The Weakness of the NDP in Federal Politics

This book seeks to explain the continuing weakness of the New Democratic party (NDP) in Canadian federal politics. It developed out of a dissatisfaction with the explanations that had hitherto been advanced to account for the party's performance. Many Canadian scholars have interpreted the NDP's weakness as a product of Canada's political culture, which is usually described as liberal with either a tory or a socialist tinge.[1] The origins of this liberal political culture are usually traced to the period of the country's founding – or to some point of cultural congealment in the distant past.[2] This approach provides contemporary political parties with little opportunity to carve their own ideological niche in society. As a result, political élites can be absolved of the responsibility for the failings of their parties.[3]

The argument in this book differs from the cultural explanations of the NDP's weakness in several respects. First of all, and most importantly, this study is guided by the assumption that political parties are able to exert influence on their direction or potential bases of support. It supposes that political parties and élites can and do play an important role in determining the parameters of political debate in a country, highlighting those cleavages which they view as pre-eminently important (and of benefit to their electoral performance) and playing down those with the opposite qualities.[4] Although this argument is not new, convincing empirical evidence has rarely been marshalled to demonstrate its efficacy. A large part of this study is therefore devoted to demonstrating both the theoretical and the empirical validity of this view of the political world. Further, a model of voting behaviour is developed which allows this dimension to be included in estimations of the determinants of voting behaviour.

Although political parties can take an active role in carving their own electoral niche, they do so within the constraints imposed by the formal rules of electoral competition, by the history of electoral politics, and by the social and political cleavages extant at any given time. Parties compete within a historical and institutional context, and that context can alter both the goals and strategies pursued by parties.

To examine the extent to which political élites can structure the content of political debate, this study focuses on union affiliation with the NDP, and the effect of affiliation on the votes of union members. This is a particularly instructive case-study because it appears at first blush to contradict the book's hypothesis. Consider that in 1961 the recently formed Canadian Labour Congress (CLC) joined with the Co-operative Commonwealth Federation (CCF), farm organizations, and other "liberally-minded Canadians" to form the NDP. Billed as the Canadian counterpart of the British Labour party,[5] the NDP was welcomed enthusiastically by the CLC as the political arm of labour, representing the first challenge since the post–World War I period by a united working class movement[6] to Canada's dominant bourgeois parties. Despite the initial euphoria, and the apparently new-found enthusiasm of organized labour in Canada for direct political action, the electoral fortunes of the NDP have not been significantly better than those of its predecessor, the CCF. If the nature of political debate is decided by élites and if, in this case, union and party élites joined to politicize economic or class cleavages in Canada, then popular support for the NDP should have dramatically outstripped support for the CCF. Until very recently, it has not.

It is argued that this case-study does not run counter to the hypothesis because the change from the CCF to the NDP did not in fact bring the party widespread support from organized labour. With respect to organizational links with labour, the NDP represented very little change from the CCF. For the most part, élites in the NDP and the union movement have not attempted to structure a strong linkage with one another. However, when that linkage did exist, it did affect the level of support the NDP received from union members.

5   The Weakness of the NDP in Federal Politics

A second way this study differs from previous ones is in the interpretation of the effect of liberalism on the NDP's base of support. Previous studies of the NDP have tended to use liberal in the sociological or cultural sense of compromising particular values, attitudes, and beliefs through which an individual's view of the political world is filtered.[7] From this perspective, a particular political culture will constrain the range of ideas considered acceptable or appropriate. Hence, many have suggested that Canada's liberal political culture has not allowed social democratic or socialist ideas and parties to flourish and is thus infertile soil for the NDP. An alternative definition of liberalism, which informs this study, can best be described as economic liberalism or the politics of public choice. This term usually is employed to describe a decision-making process defined by a maximum utility decision rule.[8] It is an evaluative or cognitive process rather than an affective one. The assumption of this study is that unions weigh the costs and benefits to themselves of their actions when making decisions. An affective like or dislike may be included in the calculation of the utility function but is only one component among many.

The investigation of the NDP's weakness in federal politics differs significantly depending upon which approach is employed. Adopting the cultural approach, the task is to identify the values, attitudes, and beliefs which predominate in society and then to investigate the period in which those attitudes took root. The major problem in such analyses is in mapping societal attitudes at a time for which data on such attitudes are notoriously sparse. Using the public choice approach, the assignment is to examine explicit and concrete decisions made by political actors at the time when those decisions are made, and at the time at which the decision rules were established. In the present analysis, the decision rules are those which govern the relationship between Canadian labour unions and the NDP, in particular the rule governing union affiliation with the party.

This book attempts to explain why the dramatic change from the CCF to the NDP – which is viewed as an explicit attempt to align the party more closely with organized labour – did not yield the anticipated increase in votes, particularly votes from union members. A satisfactory explanation must encompass both aggregate and individual levels of union support for the party. It is contended that union affiliation with the NDP has an effect on the way in which individuals view politics: namely, those who belong to union locals affiliated with the party are more likely to identify with and vote for the NDP and to view politics in class-based terms than are their counterparts whose union locals are not so affiliated.

This pattern of stable alignment among members of affiliated unions must be interpreted within the broader context of Canada's stable dealigned party system. The social roots of Canada's parties are both weak and shallow, with partisan political behaviour more strongly affected by attitudinal than socio-demographic characteristics.[9] When evaluated in the light of other socially grounded or structural determinants of political behaviour, the importance of union cues is quite impressive.

The outline of the book is straightforward. Chapter 2 presents a historical sketch of the development of the linkage between organized labour and the CCF/NDP, with particular attention to the ways in which the party tried to appeal to labour and other social groups, and to its success in doing so. Chapter 3 examines the various links that have developed between labour and the CCF and finds that each type of link, but especially direct union affiliation with the party, is relatively weak. Chapter 4 examines the rules of union affiliation with the NDP and develops a utility-maximizing model of decision-making. The decision matrix on union-party affiliation is examined, and the model is applied to available data.

Chapter 5 examines the importance of the union-party linkage on individual behaviour in a simplified model. In particular, it examines the effect of membership in a union and in an NDP-affiliated union on the political attitudes and voting behaviour of Canadians. A full reciprocal model of voting behaviour is explored in chapter 6. The reciprocal model enables the effects of long-term and short-term determinants of voting to be gauged simultaneously. The finding is that although short-term factors clearly predominate, membership in an NDP-affiliated union also is a significant predictor of NDP voting and is very robust in comparison with other long-term factors.

CHAPTER TWO

Choosing the Rules of Union-Party Affiliation: A Historical Perspective

It is often observed that nascent social democratic political parties rely on labour unions for much of their organizational and electoral support. The establishment of labour unions preceded the building of social democratic political parties in virtually all of the advanced industrial democracies, and unions were able to provide money, personnel to serve as election workers, organizers, or candidates, and symbolic or voter mobilizational support to their "political arms."[1] Typically, that support was necessary to help in overcoming the barriers or thresholds which any new party faces in seeking electoral success.

This chapter examines the links that first developed between organized labour and the CCF and which later were transferred to a large extent to the NDP. Of particular importance to this study is the development of the rules for union affiliation with the party. The transformation of the CCF into the NDP in 1961 was intended to strengthen the role of organized labour in the party. This was to be achieved by developing a more comprehensive and inclusive affiliated union structure. A measure of the success of the change in 1961 is the strength of the affiliation movement. The conclusions about the strength of the relationship between organized labour and the party are based in large part on an examination of union affiliation with the party.

The analysis focuses on three crucial periods in the development of the CCF/NDP: 1919–33, the time of the rise and decline of the Progressive party and the formation of the CCF; 1938–45, a period in which the party grew rapidly but also suffered major setbacks and in which the rules for union affiliation with the CCF were developed; and 1956–61, the years in which the formal change from the CCF to the NDP occurred. In each of these periods, leaders in the CCF/NDP regarded organized labour as only one of several important constituent groups among its supporters and attempted explicitly to avoid the perceived negative consequences of union control of the party. This strategy was the easier to pursue because organized labour itself was both organizationally fragmented and deeply divided on the matter of direct political action. Ultimately, the history of both the CCF and organized labour severely restricted the range of choices available to the individuals who were instrumental in transforming the CCF into the NDP, so that it was almost inevitable that affiliation of union locals became the only acceptable mode of linking labour unions to the party.

1919–33: THE EMERGENCE OF THE CCF

The creation of a new political party is not a natural or automatic phenomenon. Even in Canada, where a voter's psychological attachment to and electoral support for a particular political party tends to be changeable, the best predictor of any party's performance in any election remains its performance in the preceding election. For new parties to emerge, substantial and perhaps even dramatic changes must take place in the way in which Canadians think about themselves and act during an election. The less solidly entrenched is a given voter's psychological attachment and behaviour pattern, the more readily he may change his partisan preference.

It is not accidental that the most serious challenges to Canada's two-party system first arose in the Canadian west and that farmers therefore played a large role in the development of third parties. Canadians living in the prairie provinces in the early decades of the twentieth century were especially susceptible to third-party challenges to the dominant Liberals and Conservatives. Those years were characterized by tremendous growth and expansion in the west, the fruit of the National Policy developed during the 1878 election campaign. The completion of the transcontinental railway, the encouragement of immigration, the exhaustion of free land in the United States, and the development of heartier strains of grain all led to the dramatic expansion in population. The greatest increase occurred between 1901 and 1911, when the population of the prairie region grew from 419,000 to 1,328,000, an increase of 318 per cent.[2]

9 Choosing the Rules of Union-Party Affiliation

Following Confederation the Liberals and Conservatives had been slow to develop organizations among the electorate. Indeed, the Liberals took some time to build a solid parliamentary wing, and a national two-party system did not truly emerge until the election of 1896.[3] By the turn of the century the parties had become firmly rooted in the maritime provinces and in Ontario and Quebec but they were only beginning to reach into the western provinces. Neither the Liberals nor the Conservatives were very successful during this period in socializing the new settlers into identifying with and supporting the established parties. Much of the initial support, especially in the agrarian provinces of Alberta and Saskatchewan, went to the Liberal party. For example, in the Reciprocity election of 1911, 15 of the 17 members of parliament elected from Alberta and Saskatchewan were Liberals. The Conservatives' campaign, based on "No truck or trade with the Yankees," ensured that western farmers would continue to be burdened with higher prices for manufactured goods, especially agricultural implements. During the following election, in 1917, the Liberals were split over the conscription issue. Although the party's official position was to oppose conscription, thus enabling it to reinforce its support in Quebec, it also had the effect of pushing western Liberals (who favoured conscription) into the wartime coalition government, thereby blurring the distinction between Liberals and Conservatives in the west.

Thus, during the crucial period in which settlement in the region was being consolidated, neither the Liberal nor the Conservative party was able to appeal consistently to the electorate. The psychological bond which develops from continuous support for and identification with a political party was stunted in the west. To a much greater degree than voters elsewhere in the country, westerners in 1920 were open to and available for new party alliances.

The 1921 federal election was to prove decisive in breaking the two-party hold on the House of Commons. As the data in table 1 indicate, prior to that election the combined Liberal-Conservative vote averaged approximately 98 per cent of the total votes cast in national elections. In 1921, however, the Liberal-Conservative share of the vote fell to 71 per cent and, with a few notable exceptions, has remained at or below 80 per cent since that time.

In addition to the seats won by the Independent Labour party's candidates, J.S. Woodsworth and William Irvine, the Progressive

TABLE 1
Percentage Vote for the Liberal and Conservative Parties, 1878–1984

Year	Total Vote (%)	Year	Total Vote (%)
1878	98	1940	81
1882	100	1945	68
1887	100	1949	79
1891	98	1953	80
1896	91	1957	80
1900	99	1958	88
1904	99	1962	74
1908	98	1963	75
1911	99	1965	72
1917	97	1968	76
1921	71	1972	73
1925	86	1974	78
1926	91	1979	76
1930	94	1980	77
1935	75	1984	78

Source: Data from 1878–1980 are from Thorburn, *Party Politics in Canada*; data from 1984 are from Gibbins, *Conflict and Unity*. Tabulations are by the author.

party won 65 seats in the house, including almost every seat west of the Lakehead. Although it had the second largest number of seats in the House of Commons, the party refused to accept the designation of official opposition; instead, many of its members decided to support the minority Liberal government. The decision of many Progressives to support the government reflected the split among western farmers at the time. Although there was a strong and vocal radical element within the farmers' protest movement, there were also many who took a much more gradual approach to political action. Prominent among them was the leader of the Progressives, T.A. Crerar, who quickly abandoned his party to assume a cabinet position in Mackenzie King's Liberal government. The increased support for the Liberals and Conservatives in ensuing elections reflects the rather rapid demise of the Progressive party.

However, not all Progressives were inclined to abandon their party or support the government. A minority of them – including Robert Gardiner, Agnes Macphail, E.J. Garland, and Henry Spencer – joined with Woodsworth and Irvine to form the farmer-

11   Choosing the Rules of Union-Party Affiliation

labour Ginger Group in Parliament. They were joined by A.A. Heaps (labour) in 1925 and Angus MacInnis (labour) in 1930.[4] The influence this group had on the creation of a farm-labour coalition in the future CCF has been underscored by Stanley Knowles: "Although this group is usually acclaimed for the 'ginger' it provided in Parliament, for its catalytic effect on the old parties, its role in the developing political life of Canada is probably of even greater significance. It was due to the work of this group that there emerged the realization that what the workers and farmers of Canada needed was not just a collection of voices, but a group with a social philosophy, a group prepared to advocate fundamental changes so as to achieve greater equality and economic justice for all."[5]

The economic depression of the 1930s provided the stimulus for such a party. On 26 May 1932 the Ginger Group met to discuss the formation of a "Commonwealth party" to unite several of the farmer and labour factions throughout the country. Woodsworth was selected its president. During these years co-operation among various farm and labour groups was increasing throughout the country: the Western Labour Conference – which included the Independent Labour party (ILP) of Manitoba, the ILP of Saskatchewan, the Dominion Labour party of Alberta, the Socialist party of British Columbia, and the Canadian Labour party – invited representatives of farm organizations to attend its annual conference in 1931. In addition, the League for Social Reconstruction (LSR) was created in 1932 by a group of academics at McGill University and the University of Toronto and was in effect a Canadian version of the Fabian Society.

The three groups – farmers, labour, and intellectuals (the LSR and the Ginger Group) – came together at the meeting of the Western Labour Conference held in Calgary during July and August 1932. The delegates decided to launch a new party to incorporate "the three major classes in the community whose interests are the same – industrial workers, farmers, and the middle class."[6] It chose the name Co-operative Commonwealth Federation (CCF) and elected a provisional council headed by Woodsworth to draft a program and to report to the party's first conference to be held the following year.

With the assistance of Frank Underhill of the LSR, a manifesto was drafted and submitted to the CCF's inaugural conference in Regina on 19 July 1933. The Regina Manifesto was an unabashedly socialist document which was intended to unite various groups in the country within a federated party. To reinforce the fact that the party was an amalgamation of various independent groupings, the CCF subtitled itself "Farmer-Labour-Socialist." The CCF began as a federation of existing organizations which were to affiliate with provincial sections of the party. Thus, it was federated in two ways: individuals could not join the party directly as individuals, but rather had to belong to an organization which was affiliated to the party; and the affiliation of groups was to be at the provincial rather than the federal level. Because groups had to affiliate with provincial wings of the party, it was difficult, if not impossible, for national organizations to affiliate with the party. As McNaught notes: a "failure to modify this [system] was one of the chief stumbling-blocks in the way of continuous membership from the beginning of the C.B.R.E.-A.C.C.L. [Canadian Brotherhood of Railway Employees–All-Canadian Congress of Labour] union organizations,"[7] and it "produced far-reaching effects on subsequent CCF-trade union relations.[8] It also should be emphasized that the CCF's constitution provided no procedure for unions to affiliate directly with the party. By no means all unions wished to affiliate with the party. (The Trades and Labor Congress of Canada – TLC, for example, had resumed its Gomperist approach).[9] Nonetheless, even among unions that wanted to form a link with the party, affiliation was discouraged. For example, A.R. Mosher, the president of the CBRE and the ACCL (the major union central organized in opposition to the TLC), had attended the Regina conference and had won a seat on the party's executive. However, Mosher's association with the CCF caused considerable resentment among the TLC leadership, and he resigned his seat in 1936.[10]

Thus, the creation of the CCF was an attempt to form a party representing the interests of farmers, labour, and "liberally-minded Canadians," without allowing any of these groups to acquire a dominant position. This coalition was perhaps not unreasonable, given the demographic make-up of the country at the time. In 1931 28.6 per cent of the work force was employed in agriculture and 33.8 per cent in secondary production. As well, only 15.3 per cent of the non-agricultural work force was unionized; about half of these workers belonged to the TLC.[11] The CCF was perceived as a socialist party, but not a labour party, responding to the unique social and political conditions of Canada. At the close of the period, union involvement with the party remained an unresolved issue. However, it was soon to gain prominence as the party searched for organizational and financial assistance with which to contest national elections.

1938–45: UNION INVOLVEMENT WITH THE CCF

The Canadian labour movement was hit hard by the depression of the 1930s. In 1921, 16 per cent of the non-agricultural work force was unionized. By 1940 this had increased only marginally to 16.3 per cent.[12] Despite the lack of growth, the union movement was undergoing significant changes which would have an impact, among other places, on union support for the CCF.

The decision of the TLC in 1902 to exclude national unions from affiliation if an international union existed had led to the creation of a variety of alternative national and regional organizations. The creation of the Canadian and Catholic Confederation of Labour (CCCL) in 1921, for example, had the effect of virtually removing unions composed of French-speaking Quebecers from the largely English-speaking union movement. In addition, the Canadian Federation of Labour and the One Big Union directly challenged the international and craft basis of the TLC, but with limited effect. In 1921 the CBRE, led by A.R. Mosher, had been expelled from the TLC and in 1927 had joined with other English-speaking unions to form the All-Canadian Congress of Labour, with Mosher as president. The CBRE had intended to affiliate with the CCF, but no provisions could be agreed upon for affiliating a national union.[13]

Perhaps the most significant challenge to the TLC, however, had come not from organizations appearing to represent linguistic/religious and nationalist tendencies but in the form of industrial organizations. The passage of the National Labour Relations (Wagner) Act in 1935 in the United States led to increased support for industrial unions representing mostly unskilled workers in the growing industrial enterprises of mining, steelmaking, and automobile production. A number of these unions formed the Committee on Industrial Organizations within the American Federation of Labor (AFL), were suspended in 1936, and then expelled in 1937. The following year they met to form a rival organization, the Congress of Industrial Organizations (CIO), led by John L. Lewis of the coal miners' union.

Not surprisingly, because many of the workers organized by the CIO were employed by corporations with wholly owned subsidiaries (branch plants) in Canada, the struggle between the AFL and the CIO in the United States was repeated north of the border. Although opposition to the CIO was much less vigorous in Canada than in the United States, the TLC was nonetheless persuaded to conform to the policies of the AFL and to expel CIO unions. David Lewis, then national secretary of the CCF, described the situation thusly:

The most important debate [at the 1938 TLC convention, which Lewis attended] was the one on unity. Without too much controversy and without opposition from the platform, the convention decided to maintain labour unity and to continue to welcome the membership of CIO unions ... About a month later, the AFL issued a ukase to the effect that the Canadian unions must "conform with the policies of the Federation and expel all its CIO affiliates." The leaders of the TLC did not even protest ...; they proceeded to suspend all CIO unions and the TLC convention held in ... 1939 confirmed their action. The Canadian labour movement was thus split contrary to its wishes by order of the AFL leaders in the United States.[14]

Following their expulsion from the TLC, the CIO affiliates in Canada held a convention in conjunction with the ACCL in 1940, formed the Canadian Congress of Labour (CCL), and elected Mosher as president. From the beginning the CCL was tied much more closely to the CCF than the TLC had been – in part because prominent CCFers were instrumental in the organizing drives of industrial unions.[15] Lewis wrote at the time: "From the CCF point of view [the] merger may prove of very great value ... [T]he new organization is likely to become a staunch supporter of the CCF."[16] Indeed, more than most CCFers, Lewis had been convinced of the need to bring organized labour into the party, and instrumental in solidifying the ties with labour.[17] Right from the start of his tenure as national secretary he had attempted to encourage labour's support of the CCF. In addition to his involvement in the creation of the CCL, he paid frequent calls on labour leaders to obtain financial assistance. As he notes in his memoirs:

"From my British and continental studies as a young student, I had always been convinced that it is impossible to build a mass social democratic party without the organized labour movement as its base ... There is ... a social and economic affinity between the two which has brought them together politically in other western countries and should do so in Canada."[18]

However, the manner in which labour unions and a social democratic party are brought together is important in defining the nature of their relationship. At the time of the founding of the CCF, organized labour was to be one of several groups represented by the party. The party's organizational principle was that it was a co-ordinating body for affiliated farmers' organizations, labour and socialist parties, and CCF clubs. Although it was anticipated that labour unions would affiliate with the party, no formal rules (governing dues payable, representation, or indeed whether union centrals, federations, or locals could affiliate) had been established.

This situation had begun to change in 1936 when the CCF's national convention adopted a resolution calling on its members "to associate themselves actively with the organizations of their trade, industry and profession." The overtures to labour became more forthright in 1937 and 1938 when the National Council of the CCF was urged "to facilitate the affiliation of economic groups such as co-operatives, farm organizations and trade unions."[19]

Then, quite unexpectedly, and with no previous contact with the CCF, District 26 of the United Mine Workers (UMW) – representing coal miners in Nova Scotia and New Brunswick, with its headquarters on Cape Breton Island – voted on 15 August 1938 to affiliate with the CCF. It thus became necessary for the CCF to stipulate the manner in which economic groups could affiliate with the party, a task undertaken by David Lewis and Angus MacInnis.

As Lewis notes, the British Labour party provided the model for union affiliation with the CCF.[20] For example, the affiliated organizations had to accept the constitution and program of the party; union delegates to CCF bodies must not be supporters of any other party; and affiliated organizations were required to pay per-capita monthly membership dues.[21] However, affiliation would differ in several important respects from the British model. First, affiliation was to take place at the level of union locals rather than federations or national and regional councils, even though the first union to vote for affiliation (UMW District 26) was a district council of UMW locals in the Atlantic region. In addition, both a block vote at party conventions and block representation on the party council were rejected in favour of a system of representation which gave affiliated unions less representation per capita than constituency organizations had. The rationale for this decision was that the party was not to be a party of organized labour. As Lewis notes:

The structure of the CCF placed control where it belonged: in the members and in the leadership of the party ... It is true that labour people played an important role in the CCF, but to the extent that trade unions as such were directly affiliated ... their delegates could not control national or provincial conventions or councils ... The suggestion that unions "controlled" the CCF was sheer fiction ...
[The British practice of block voting was] totally inappropriate for a party like the CCF in a country like Canada, where considerations of regional balance and the strength of the farmer's voice had to be given as much attention as the place of affiliated unions.[22]

No additional union locals affiliated with the CCF between 1938 and 1942. However, there were dramatic improvements in the party's electoral fortunes in the early 1940s, and, after 1942, a rapid rise in the number of locals affiliated with the party.

The first major success for the CCF occurred in the 1941 provincial election in British Columbia. The party won a plurality of votes and the second largest number of seats (14, compared with 21 for the Liberals and 12 for the Conservatives). The success in British Columbia was soon followed by a series of breakthroughs for the CCF in by-elections and general elections. During 1942 and 1943 ten provincial and federal by-elections were held throughout the country. The CCF won eight of them. By far the most important of these, for its impact on the growth of the CCF, was that of 9 February 1942 in the federal riding of York South in Ontario – traditionally a Conservative bastion. Arthur Meighen, who had twice been prime minister in the 1920s, had once again been selected leader of the Conservative party and was seeking election to the House of Commons as a "parachute" candidate. The Liberal party decided not to contest the seat in deference to the leader of the official opposition, but the CCF ran J.W. Noseworthy, a local high school teacher and member of the executive of the provincial teachers' federation. To the surprise of most observers, Noseworthy defeated Meighen in an election which "galvanized the CCF."[23]

The York South by-election foreshadowed the spectacular showing of the CCF in the Ontario provincial election of 4 August 1943, in which the party moved from 5.7 per cent of the popular vote and no seats in the 1937 election to 31.6 per cent of the popular vote and 34 (of 90) seats in the legislative assembly.[24] Without minimizing the significant gains made by the CCF in the 1943 Ontario election – the party's vote had increased from 87,000 to 415,000 in one election period – it should be noted that voter turnout in 1943 (58.3 per cent) was the fourth lowest ever in the province, higher only than that in the 1923 (52.9 per cent), 1929 (56.6 per cent), and 1981 (58.0 per cent) elections. Turnout had dropped 13 percentage points from the previous election and would regain almost 14 percentage points in the following election. Although some of the drop-off may be ascribed to the fact that it was a wartime election, results from other provincial elections held during the war typically show a drop-off of approximately 5 per cent. A more plausible explanation for the unusually low turnout in Ontario in 1943 was the unpopularity of the Liberal government (the Liberals lost 48 of their 63 seats and almost 400,000 of their 773,000 votes) and the inability of either the Conservatives (who gained 15 seats on their previous 23 while dropping 150,000 of their 620,000 votes) or the CCF to capture more of those disenchanted voters. Thus, although the 1943 Ontario provincial election was catalytic for the CCF's prospects, some of the forces which shaped this positive showing would forestall the further growth of the party in the province.

The perception that the CCF was on the brink of electoral takeoff was reinforced by the party's landslide victory in the Saskatchewan election of 15 June 1944. In the 1938 provincial election the CCF had won 21.5 per cent of the popular vote and 10 of 52 seats in the legislature, compared with 38 seats for the governing Liberals. In 1944 the CCF increased its share of the popular vote to 53.4 per cent and captured 47 seats to become the first avowedly social democratic government on the North American continent.

By 1944, which marked the apex of power and popular support for the CCF, not only was it the government in Saskatchewan, but it formed the official opposition in the other four provinces west of the Ottawa river. In provinces east of Ontario the party's fortunes were more modest: it had no seats in Prince Edward Island and New Brunswick, held 3 of 30 seats in Nova Scotia between 1941 and 1945, and had won a single seat in the legislative assembly in Quebec in 1944 – only to have its representative switch to the Liberal party the following year. Nonetheless, the party's overall prospects looked bright.

In conjunction with the CCF's improved electoral performance, its links with organized labour were growing stronger and broader. In June 1942, following the York South by-election, a convention of the Trade Union Committee of the Ontario CCF, representing both TLC and CCL unions, passed a resolution urging unions to affiliate with the CCF and to endorse the party as the political arm of the trade union movement. At its annual convention the following year the CCL passed a resolution endorsing the CCF "as the political arm of labour in Canada, and recommended to all affiliated ... unions that they affiliate with the CCF."[25] However, the drive for affiliation was confined mainly to Ontario and, despite an initial leap in the rate of affiliation, there never were significant numbers of union locals affiliated with the party. For example, affiliation with the CCF reached its zenith in 1944 – approximately 100 locals with 50,000 members. This represented approximately 6.9 per cent of the 724,000 union members in Canada. By 1945 the affiliation movement had ground to a halt in Ontario. The number of affiliated union locals nationwide fell to 71 in 1947, and to 44 in 1952, and then remained relatively stable until the formation of the NDP in 1961.[26]

A number of explanations have been offered for the failure of the affiliation movement after 1945. First of all, in a number of unions, and especially in such key ones as the United Automobile Workers (UAW), the International Brotherhood of Electrical Workers (IBEW), the Mine Mill Workers, and the International Woodworkers of America (IWA), communists actively discouraged affiliation with the CCF.[27] The effect of communist influence is stated cogently by Morton: "The CCL endorsement was a precedent of enormous importance but of little immediate value. Within the CCL and in all its major industrial unions, a bitter remorseless struggle for control was soon raging between Communist leaders and their opponents – most of them militant CCFers ... While they held control, the Communists effectively prevented support for their CCF rivals ... Even where they had been defeated in all but a handful of unions, the scars remained."[28]

Secondly, the example of the approach of the CIO unions to politics in the United States, which centred on providing organizational and material support for desirable candidates while maintaining independence from any one party, as well as direct pressure from international headquarters, may have inhibited Canadian unions from affiliating. Thirdly, the increasingly close ties between the TLC leadership and the Liberal government may have forced the CCL to re-evaluate its policy of building closer ties with the CCF, especially once the latter ceased to make advances electorally.[29]

The electoral successes of the CCF came to a dramatic halt in 1945. As Lewis notes: "We did not realize it at the time but, in retrospect, it seems clear to me that 1945 was the year which decided the fate of the CCF."[30] In both the Ontario provincial election and the federal election (held on 4 and 11 June, respectively), the CCF's performance was much worse than anticipated. In Ontario, the party fell from 34 to 8 seats and its proportion of the popular vote dropped from 31.6 to 22.4 per cent. The Liberal party (with 11 seats) became the official opposition to the Conservative government (66 seats). The CCF's popular vote declined only marginally, from 415,000 to 396,000, but turnout had increased from 58.3 to 72.1 per cent of the electorate. Thus, although the Ontario provincial election results were disheartening for the party, and were to have a significant impact on the federal election one week later, they can be explained in part by the fact that the 1943 results overstated the party's popular support among the electorate as a whole. Many of those who were dissatisfied with the Liberals and Conservatives in 1943 chose not to vote rather than to support the CCF. When the Conservatives were more popular in 1945, they received a disproportionate share of the votes of the "transient" electorate[31] – those who had not voted in 1943, but voted in 1945 – and increased their popular vote by over 300,000 to 781,000.

The federal election proved even more disappointing for the CCF. It increased its share of the vote from 8 to 16 per cent and its seats from 8 to 28 (of 245). After the significant gains made by the party between 1941 and 1944, however, these results were well below its anticipated performance. The disappointment was compounded by the distribution of the party's support. It won only 14 per cent of the vote and no seats in Ontario and only a single seat (on Cape Breton Island) east of Manitoba. By far the largest number of seats it captured were in Saskatchewan (18 of 21 from that province).

Gad Horowitz suggests that the poor showing of the CCF in the 1945 elections had two effects on the affiliation movement: union enthusiasm for the CCF diminished and CCF enthusiasm for the labour movement waned.[32] However, union support for the party, as measured by rate of affiliation, had never been strong, in part because the CCF had sought explicitly to minimize union influence in the party. Moreover it is important to remember that most of the party's members of parliament were from rural, largely agrarian, western constituencies. To the extent that a party's representatives influence the character of the party, the distribution of electoral support for the CCF might be thought to ensure that agrarian interests would be the more significant throughout its existence and the cultivation of labour of less importance.

With the 1945 elections, the CCF's growth ceased, and the party entered a period of stasis and, eventually, decline. At the federal level, its share of the popular vote declined from the high point of 16 per cent in 1945, to 13 per cent (13 seats) in 1949, 11 per cent in 1953 (23 seats) and 1957 (25 seats), and finally to 9 per cent and 8 seats in 1958, the last election contested by the CCF.[33] At the provincial level between 1945 and 1960, the party won no seats in Prince Edward Island, Newfoundland, or Quebec, fewer than 5 seats in Nova Scotia and Alberta, 21 seats in Ontario in 1948 (but lost all but a handful subsequently), from 5 to 11 seats in Manitoba, and remained the official opposition in British Columbia and the government in Saskatchewan.

However, by the middle to late 1950s, significant changes were taking place in the labour movement, both organizationally and with respect to its position on direct political action. Moreover, the CCF's poor performance in the 1958 national election convinced many in the party that the time had arrived to strengthen its ties with organized labour. Although these changes ultimately led to the formation of the NDP, the character of the new party, as well as its linkage with organized labour, was to be influenced strongly by the historical development of the CCF.

21   Choosing the Rules of Union-Party Affiliation

1956–61: THE FOUNDING OF THE NDP

After an eighteen-year division between craft and industrial unions in the United States, the AFL and CIO merged in 1955 to form the AFL-CIO. This merger cleared the way for a merger of their Canadian counterparts, the TLC and the CCL, to form the Canadian Labour Congress (CLC) in 1956. Although the CCF had developed close ties with the CCL – the latter had reaffirmed its 1943 resolution calling the CCF "the political arm of labour" at each subsequent convention – the party's relationship with the TLC had always been much weaker. Horowitz describes the TLC policy toward political action thusly:

The TLC's political policy was not, like that of the AFL, a *positive* policy of support for capitalism *against* socialism. Gompers Canadianized is not an atheist, but an agnostic – not an anti-socialist, but a non-socialist susceptible to socialist influence; not an opponent of labour or socialist parties, but an opponent of *union* involvement in their activities ... The TLC's non-partisanship did not mean a preference for Liberals and/or Conservatives against socialists. It meant no preference for anyone; "no politics" at all.[34]

The different approaches of the CCL and the TLC to political action were viewed by many as a potential stumbling block to their merger. Intense negotiations between the two congresses, at which "leading CCF representatives were always present,"[35] led to an agreement that the matter of endorsing the CCF would best be left off the agenda of the new congress' inaugural convention. Instead, the CLC adopted two resolutions which were to provide guidelines for future action. In essence, they entailed creating a Political Education Committee whose tasks were to assist affiliates in carrying out their programmes of political education and to urge affiliates to enter into discussions with other economic organizations to co-ordinate both legislative and political action with the CCF or other parties. Lewis notes the significance of the latter resolution: "No one was fooled by the mention of other political parties ... The aim of the resolution was obviously to explore the possibility of a new political alignment. The statement gave the Congress leaders as well as the Political Education Committee authority to enter into serious discussion with the CCF about future relationships. This was welcomed by the CCF; indeed, we had hoped for just such a development.[36]

Thus, with the unification of the English-speaking union movement came the beginnings of agreement on a more direct approach to politics. As a result of the ensuing discussions between the CCF leadership and the Political Education Committee of the CLC, the decision was made to involve organized labour more fully in direct political action. The following CLC convention, in 1958, passed a resolution calling for "a broadly based people's political movement, which embraces the CCF, the Labour Movement, farm organizations, professional people and other liberally-minded persons" and instructed its Executive Council to enter into discussion with those groups "to formulate a constitution and a program for such a political instrument."[37]

In short, the CLC was calling for the creation of a new political party in which labour would fulfil the role initially envisioned for it in the CCF. For its part, the CCF was also moving towards accepting a greater role for labour in the party than had hitherto developed. For example, at its 1956 convention the CCF had adopted the Winnipeg Declaration of Principles, which replaced the Regina Manifesto as a statement of the party's philosophy. In contrast to the overall tone of the Regina Manifesto, which sought to "replace the present capitalist system" and which referred to the capitalist mode of production as "the cancer which is eating at the heart of our society," the Winnipeg Declaration represented a significant moderation of rhetoric, if not policy. For example, the declaration begins by noting: "The aim of the Co-operative Commonwealth Federation is the establishment in Canada by democratic means of a co-operative commonwealth in which the supplying of human needs and enrichment of human life shall be the primary purpose of our society. Private property and corporate power must be subordinated to social planning." In place of the Regina Manifesto's conclusion that "no C.C.F. Government will rest content until it has eradicated capitalism," the Winnipeg Declaration concluded that: "the CCF will not rest content until every person in this land and in all lands is able to enjoy equality and freedom, a sense of human dignity, and an opportunity to live a rich and meaningful life as a citizen of a free and peaceful world.[38]

Although the CCF had been moving towards forging stronger links with the labour movement, the 1958 federal election proved

23 Choosing the Rules of Union-Party Affiliation

a stimulus. That election occurred less than a year after the 1957 election which had returned a minority Conservative government, the first Conservative government since 1935. Led by the western populist, John Diefenbaker, the Conservatives had captured 21 of 70 seats west of Ontario in 1957 compared with 22 for the CCF. However, in 1958, the Conservatives won 65 of 70 seats in the four western provinces compared to 5 for the CCF. Even more devastating for the CCF, M.J. Coldwell, the party's leader since the death of Woodsworth in 1942, lost his seat, as did Stanley Knowles, one of the party's leading luminaries, in the riding of Winnipeg North Centre which had been held by the party since 1921 (first by Woodsworth and then by Knowles). Overall, the Conservatives received 54 per cent of the popular vote (the second largest proportion ever won), and 208 of 265 seats in the house, the largest majority of seats ever won. For the CCF the inability of the party to improve its electoral performance during a period of collapse for the Liberal party was significant. The realization that the party would not automatically replace the Liberals convinced many in the CCF that the time for change had arrived.

At its biennial convention in 1958, held only months after the CLC's call for a new political party and the Conservative election victory, the CCF authorized its National Council and National Executive to enter into discussions with the CLC, the CCCL, interested farm organizations, and "other like minded groups and individuals," with the prospect of forming a new party. Several months earlier the CLC and the CCF had established a "joint political committee," chaired by Stanley Knowles, to explore further the CLC's new party resolution.[39] Knowles also had been elected a vice-president of the CLC at its April 1958 convention and thus served as a major link between the party and the congress.

Shortly after the CCF convention, the joint political committee was renamed the National Committee for the New Party (NCNP), and representatives of labour, the CCF, farm organizations and, after 1959, New Party clubs, were encouraged to participate. However, no farm organizations participated actively, and to the extent that farmers were involved in founding the NDP, it was as individual members of CCF constituency organizations or New Party clubs. After two years of extensive discussions throughout the country, both the CLC and the CCF conventions of 1960 firmly committed themselves to the formation of a new party. The party's founding convention was held from 31 July through 4 August 1961, at which time it adopted the name New Democratic party and approved a constitution.

Although the NDP constitution provides for the affiliation of farm organizations, the change from the CCF to the NDP was intended to bring organized labour rather than farm organizations more fully into the party fold. In fact, no farm organizations ever have been affiliated with the NDP. The balance which the CCF intended to institute between labour, farmers, and "liberally-minded individuals" was altered; the NDP combined organized labour and individual members represented through constituency associations, with the balance of power held by the latter.

To maintain that balance (that is, to guard against union domination), the NDP adopted the position taken previously by the CCF that there would be no block voting at party conventions and no block representation on the national executive of the party.[40] In both, each delegate would be entitled to a single vote. Further, representation at conventions differs for constituency and affiliated organizations. For the former, delegates are allocated according to the following formula: "One delegate for 50 members or less, one delegate for each additional 50 members or major fraction thereof up to a total of 200 members, and one delegate for each additional 100 members or major fraction thereof." Delegates for affiliated organizations, however, are apportioned as follows: "Each affiliated local group or organization, and each affiliated local, lodge or branch of a group or organization ... shall be entitled to one delegate for the first 1,000 members or less, and one delegate for each additional 1,000 members or major fraction thereof."[41]

The consistency of the CCF and NDP on affiliation rules underscores the more general consistency of views held by the two parties. In his study of the Manitoba CCF, Nelson Wiseman argues: "Although [Howard Pawley] lost the fight to save the CCF, his fears [of union domination] were allayed because the NDP was not all that different from the CCF. In Manitoba, as in Canada, the NDP's leaders, policies, and base of electoral support barely changed in the 1960s from the CCF experience of the 1950s."[42] In theory, the NDP welcomes affiliation of national, regional, or local labour organizations, but in practice only the affiliation of local ones is encouraged. Only local organizations ever have affiliated with the party, a legacy of the relationship between organized labour and the CCF. Indeed, the creation of the NDP, with the assistance of organized labour, was seen by many in the party as the achievement of the original purpose of the CCF. In the words of Lewis, "the CCF had decided to yield its name and position in order to revert to its original intention."[43] Furthermore, as Horowitz notes, the constitutional principles of the NDP "do not represent a startling departure from the provisions of the CCF itself ... What is new is not provision for affiliation – that existed in the CCF – but the determination that it cease to be a dead letter, the determination actually to build up a large affiliated-union section."[44]

Some have argued that even within the NDP, union affiliation has not been an issue of central concern to the party. As Wiseman notes: "Although the overwhelming number of Manitoba union locals did not affiliate with the NDP in the 1960s this did not particularly concern party or union leaders. Affiliation fees were a small fraction of union contributions. For the provincial party, affiliation was primarily a symbolic act."[45] But this is precisely why union affiliation is a matter of such importance to the party. Affiliation fees contribute a very modest proportion of the NDP's revenues. The main purpose of affiliation is to provide a "cue" to union members that there is an important link between the party and organized labour. Chapters 5 and 6 explore in detail the extent to which this cue is effective and conclude that without a strong affiliation movement, the positive cue is lacking.

This is all the more ironic because the attempt to align the party more closely with organized labour has ensured that the party will bear the negative consequences of perceived labour domination, while reaping very little in the way of a behavioural cue. As Morton notes: "The charge of labour domination supplanted the older bogeys of socialism as a favourite weapon for opponents ... The leadership had designed a constitutional structure which refuted any logical charge of trade union tyranny and assumed that that would suffice."[46] But it has not proved sufficient to deter the charge of union domination. The NDP is saddled with the burden of its relationship with organized labour without receiving many of the benefits that such a relationship might provide. A strong affiliation movement appears to be out of the reach of the party, in part because of the reasons outlined above, but only in part. Although it is a fact that communist influence prevented some unions from affiliating, as did the constitutional structure of some international unions, it also is a fact that the rate of affiliation is very low even among union locals whose national bodies actively support the party. The next chapters explore why so few union locals have affiliated with the NDP.

CHAPTER THREE

Measuring the Union Link to the NDP

The formal change from the CCF to the NDP was intended to link the party much more closely with organized labour. The change did not involve forming a new alignment, but rather using the renewed labour unity provided by the creation of the CLC as an opportunity to solidify the linkage which already had been developed through the CCF. It also provided the party with an opportunity to shed its image as a party responding to the economic depression of the 1930s in favour of one capable of tackling the issues facing a country in the midst of postwar prosperity and unprecedented industrial growth.

The varied and complex links that exist between the party and organized labour can be divided into three general types: personnel links, union contributions to the party's revenues, and direct union affiliation with the party. To understand the overall relationship between organized labour and the NDP, this chapter explores these aspects of that relationship.

PERSONNEL RELATIONS

The personnel linkage between organized labour and the NDP is amorphous and difficult to measure. Links may be formal and entrenched in the party's constitution, they may be informal and established by convention, or they may be informal, ad hoc, and subject to considerable variation over time. Additionally, the unionist involved in the NDP may participate on behalf of a central labour organization (such as the CLC or a provincial federation of labour), as a representative of a national or international union, such as the Canadian Automobile Workers (CAW), on behalf of an affiliated or unaffiliated union local, including directly chartered locals, or purely as an individual.

The party's *formal* personnel links with labour began to emerge in the years leading up to the creation of the NDP. The National Committee for the New Party (NCNP) played a large role in formalizing the nature of union participation in the new party's councils and in deciding upon the rules of union affiliation.[1]

The formal union representation on party decision-making bodies is outlined in the constitution. Article v.2 declares that the party's convention is the "supreme governing body of the Party and shall have final authority in all matters of federal policy, programme and constitution." The allocation of delegate seats at a convention thus provides an insight into the depth and breadth of the union-party linkage. There are a number of delegate categories at NDP conventions. All members of the Federal Council and the federal parliamentary caucus are entitled to delegate status. Constituency associations, through the provincial wings of the party, are accorded delegates based on their size and according to the formula set out in the constitution (see chapter 2). In addition, delegates are awarded to the youth wing of the party and to two categories of union delegates: central labour[2] and affiliated organizations.

The party was careful to ensure that the formula for allocating convention delegates would guarantee that labour would not dominate the convention. For example, at the 1987 federal convention, 240 of the 1391 delegates (17.3 per cent) were from affiliated unions and 72 (5.2 per cent) were from central labour.[3] The 1987 data, where delegates with union credentials made up almost one-quarter of the total delegates, are consistent with the general pattern of union representation at party conventions. Union delegates as a proportion of total delegates were 19.7 per cent in 1973, 25.8 per cent in 1975, 22.5 per cent in 1977, 24.0 per cent in 1979, and 17.4 per cent in 1981. Even at the 1971 convention which elected David Lewis as leader and in which the role of organized labour in the party was being challenged directly by the Waffle candidate, James Laxer, organized labour could muster only 32.3 per cent of all delegates.[4]

However, caution should be used in interpreting the data on delegate status at party conventions. Some delegates may be very active union members, but appear under another delegate category if, for example, they also belong to caucus, council, the youth wing, or a constituency association. Thus, the number of delegates who are union members always exceeds those who have union delegate status. Conversely, it should be obvious that the role of labour in the party is strongest when unionists are unified in their outlook and orientation, a characteristic which organized labour in Canada is seldom accused of possessing. The effect of labour representation at conventions is accurately conveyed by Wiseman in his study of the Manitoba NDP: "The change in composition of delegates from CCF [to NDP] conventions was more apparent than real. The new affiliation provisions permitted many CCFers to appear as labour delegates ... It is doubtful that more than 5 of the Manitoba delegation [to the NDP founding convention] would have been ineligible to attend had it been simply another CCF convention."[5] Furthermore, and along a more substantive vein, he notes that the resolutions presented by organized labour to the conventions of the Manitoba NDP "were almost always restricted to [labour's] specific legislative concerns."[6]

In the two-year period between conventions, the party is governed by the Federal Council, which meets at least twice a year at the call of the executive. As with the convention delegates, there are several categories of council member, including the federal party's 12 officers, 20 members selected from the federal convention, 2 members from the federal caucus, 40 members from the provincial parties' table officers, 30 members selected from the provincial parties' conventions, and 12 members representing the largest affiliated organizations. In addition the council may appoint up to 5 additional members. Therefore, total membership on the Federal Council numbers between 116 and 121, of which 12 (approximately 10 per cent) are specifically allocated to affiliated unions. The Federal Council invariably has more than 12 union officials as members at any given time, but their place on council is not formally determined by their union status.

Between meetings of the Federal Council the executive has the authority to conduct and administer the affairs and business of the party. The executive consists of the 12 officers (leader, president and associate president, 8 vice-presidents, and treasurer) and 14 members elected by and from the Federal Council. Unlike council members and convention delegates, there are no specific provisions for the officers or executive of the party to have union representatives among them. A literal reading of the party's constitution would suggest that these offices could be filled without any union representation at all. But such a reading of the party's constitution would lead to a mistaken interpretation and would be analogous to a literal reading of the Constitution Act 1867. That document refers to the cabinet as the Queen's Privy Council, whose members are summoned from time to time by the crown. In fact, Canada's constitutional conventions require that the governor general make appointments to the Privy Council on the recommendation of the prime minister. There is a further constitutional convention that the prime minister will ensure adequate representation within cabinet from the various regions as well as from religious, ethnic, linguistic, and gender groups. The constitutional convention is less clear in defining what constitutes adequate representation for each group, but it does ensure that the prime minister will remain sensitive to group representation in the selection process.

For the NDP, there is likewise a strong convention making for adequate union representation within the inner councils of the party. Typically, there are prominent union representatives on the party executive and among the table officers. Although there is no definitive understanding of the number of union representatives considered to be adequate, it is typical to find that labour leaders occupy approximately 20 to 25 per cent of the executive and officer positions.[7]

The personnel links between organized labour and the NDP extend well beyond membership in the formal councils of the party. As early as the 1940s the CCF was encouraging labour unions, and especially CCL unions, to create their own political action committees, a step which the CCL itself had taken in the early 1940s.[8] The CLC has maintained a Committee on Political Education (COPE) almost since its inception, and although small in size and resources (3 full-time staff), it maintains continual contact and communication with the party. It also attempts to co-ordinate the political activities of its affiliates and encourages union locals to affiliate with the NDP.

Labour unions also have provided the party with both personnel and organizational resources to conduct party conventions and contest elections. Desmond Morton describes one of the important contributions of labour to the party's founding convention: "CCF conventions had been gatherings of only a few hundred delegates, meeting annually in hotel ballrooms and halls. For the Founding Convention, trade unionists contributed their organizing expertise. From the decorations to the labour troubadours ... it looked and was professional. The new image was being fashioned."9 In an era in which the electronic media were playing a greater role in delivering "politics" to Canadians, and "image" was becoming a more important political commodity, the organizational resources of labour became of greater importance to the party.

The campaign techniques which the NDP began to develop in the 1960s also placed a premium on personnel and organizational resources. The party's major campaign innovation was developed during a by-election in the Toronto constituency of Riverdale in 1964. In short, the technique involved massive door-to-door canvassing throughout the campaign, with a party worker visiting a voter's home three and four times before the election.[10] This technique appealed to the NDP, not only because it was relatively cost-effective, but also because organized labour could provide the army of canvassers needed for such a labour-intensive effort.

There are many other minor ways in which labour contributes to the personnel and organizational needs of the party. Many unionists serve as table officers of constituency associations, and many constituency associations hold their monthly meetings in union halls. Unions often provide personnel and vehicles on election day and other material support to assist in campaigns to get out the vote.

Given its wide range, it is not possible to measure the overall personnel contribution of labour to the party. Although labour does make a significant contribution, there are also very real limits on its contribution as an organization. On the party's decision-making bodies, labour is not able to provide more than a minority voice, albeit a significant one. Informally, the types of contributions are wide ranging, but only some of them are sponsored by the organizations themselves. Much of the overlap in personnel between the union movement and the NDP lies in individual Canadians, acting not in their capacity as union officials, but rather as individuals exercising their democratic rights. And this type of support may owe very little to the formal alliance that emerged between organized labour and the NDP.

FINANCIAL CONTRIBUTIONS

The financial relationship between organized labour and the NDP is only somewhat more straightforward and measurable than the personnel linkage. The passage of the Canada Elections Act in 1974 has, among other things, shed light on the financing of candidates and political parties in Canada. Parties are now required to submit audited financial statements each year to the chief electoral officer, which are then made public, and to disclose in their reports the names of all persons or organizations donating $100 or more to a candidate or party. The legislation also introduced a system of public funding for political parties by providing tax credits for political contributions.[11]

Despite the mandatory public disclosure of revenues, it is not possible to determine definitively the various sources of NDP funding. The party's unique organizational structure complicates its financial arrangements considerably. The NDP is a federated party in which there is no complete separation between federal and provincial levels.[12] Membership in the NDP is available through the provincial wings of the party, and provincial membership brings with it automatic membership in the federal party. It is not possible to join the federal wing of the NDP without joining a provincial wing. And, because the party's constitution precludes membership of other political parties by its members, one cannot even belong to the federal Liberals or Progressive Conservatives while being a member of a provincial wing of the New Democrats. This provision sets the NDP apart from both the Liberal and the Conservative parties, neither of which prohibits members of other federal parties from joining and both of which maintain much clearer distinctions between their federal and provincial wings.

One of the implications of the NDP's membership policies is that the federal and provincial wings have a much closer and more intertwined financial relationship than is true of the other major parties. This fiscal overlap affects the way in which the party's revenues are reported to the chief electoral officer. The returns of registered parties report the contributions each party receives for a given fiscal period under a number of headings. Although the categories have changed somewhat over time, typically they include contributions from individuals, business or commercial organizations, governments, trade unions, other organizations, and miscellaneous. Since 1974, the NDP has been the only party to list the revenues of the provincial wings of the party. It does so even though these funds generally fall under the jurisdiction of the provincial wings. The fiscal relationship is complicated, however, because the federal party levies a 15-per-cent tax on all revenues raised by the provincial sections and, during election campaigns, it can also exact an assessment from each provincial section, thereby effectively controlling the expenditure of at least some of these funds.[13] However, and this is the issue that is most problematic in calculating the relative weight of union contributions, the provincial revenues are not broken down according to source. Consequently, this discussion of the proportion of funds which the party receives from union sources will be limited to the funds raised and controlled by the federal wing of the NDP.

The data on the NDP's revenues from 1979 to 1986 are presented in table 2.[14] Because conclusions about the size of union financial contributions will vary according to whether federal or federal-provincial data are used, both are presented. Focusing on federal revenues first, table 2 shows that the party's revenues grew considerably, although not consistently, from $4.7 million to $7.8 million annually between 1979 and 1986. The lion's share of the funding in each year came from individuals contributing to the party. (Parenthetically, throughout this entire period more individuals contributed to the New Democratic party than to any other federal party in Canada.) Overall, individual contributions ranged from a low of 54.4 per cent of the federal party's revenues in 1979 to a high of 83.6 per cent in 1983. As well, there has been a reasonably steady growth in contributions by individuals over time.[15]

Contributions from trade unions to the NDP are of two types: annual dues paid by unions affiliated with the party, and other donations made outside the formal affiliation mechanism. In a pattern similar to that for individual contributions, union contributions through affiliation fees have grown steadily and consistently in absolute terms and have remained remarkably stable in relative terms. The data also indicate the marginality of affiliation fees to the overall fiscal outlook of the party. At no point during this period have affiliation dues constituted as much as 10 per cent of the party's revenues; instead they have ranged from a high of 9.0 per cent in 1981 to a low of 5.0 per cent in 1983.

The major variation in financial contributions to the NDP over time is in the category of "other union contributions." The very

TABLE 2
New Democratic Party Revenue, 1979–86

Source	1979	1980	1981	1982	1983	1984	1985	1986
Individual	$2,584,536	$2,817,387	$2,868,724	$3,774,971	$4,998,350	$4,156,000	$4,611,704	$5,036,131
Business/Commercial	169,298	91,369	109,062	144,324	41,432	51,665	58,417	177,960
Government	97,752	26,828	39,619	143,358	67,155	181,010	69,890	74,585
Union								
Affiliation Dues	319,196	338,271	353,300	316,106	299,688	417,480	566,833	633,928
Other Union	1,382,420	1,364,557	161,886	157,033	336,851	1,741,575	302,568	538,856
Other Organizations	5,523*	7,678*	2,367	1,320	2,590	1,950	34,644	4,642
Interest	46,417	61,460	102,167	123,316	77,710	141,678	105,863	127,292
Miscellaneous	136,139	212,897	218,687	106,054	147,755	665,545	534,397	391,269
Provincial Election Rebates	—	—	—	—	—	—	—	810,995
FEDERAL TOTAL	4,741,281	4,920,447	3,855,812	4,766,482	5,971,531	7,356,903	6,284,316	7,795,658
Provincial Revenues	1,278,885	1,810,210	2,146,770	2,341,715	2,697,121	3,155,793	3,867,695	6,843,667
TOTAL	6,020,166	6,100,657	6,002,582	7,108,197	8,668,652	10,512,696	10,152,011	14,639,325

* Includes public corporations and unincorporated organizations.
Source: Canada, Elections Canada, Registered Party Fiscal Period Returns, selected years.

clear pattern is for contributions from unions to increase dramatically during election years, but to fall off equally dramatically in non-election years. Union contributions to the NDP's election war chest come from many different sources. The most significant donations tend to be from the headquarters of national or international unions (contributions in 1984 included $122,500 from the Steelworkers, over $40,000 from the Food and Commercial Workers, $29,000 from the Service Employees Union, among many others) as well as from national, provincial, or regional labour councils.

It is very significant that during election years organized labour is able to contribute between $1.5 million and $2.1 million to the federal NDP as well as additional funds to the provincial sections which are then turned over to the federal office. However, these data must be interpreted in light of two other fiscal realities; even at their high point during an election year, union contributions are outweighed by individual contributions, and they are significantly outweighed by individual donations in non-election years. In addition, although the $2.1 million contributed to the NDP in 1984 enabled the party to marshall an effective national election campaign, the amount pales in comparison to the $5.3 million and $11.0 million which corporate sponsors contributed to the Liberal and Progressive Conservatives parties, respectively.

UNION AFFILIATION WITH THE NDP

We have noted that the NDP did not introduce the idea of direct union affiliation with the party. The first union had affiliated with the CCF in 1938, and there had been continuous provisions for union affiliation thereafter. However, union affiliation with the CCF had always remained low. Nelson Wiseman describes the situation in 1952: "CCF success in attracting trade unionists was not great. In 1952 there were less than 15,000 affiliated unionists in Canada and 10,000 of these were from the miners' union in Nova Scotia. There were no union affiliates at all, at that date, from Manitoba. The 2 cent per month per member affiliate fee, whenever and wherever collected, provided only marginal income for the CCF; the Manitoba party collected $80 from this source in 1945 and $50 in 1950."[16] The highest level of affiliation with the CCF had occurred in 1944, at which time 100 unions with approximately 50,000 members were affiliated with the party. This number constituted approximately 6.9 per cent of the unionized work force in that year.[17] By the early 1950s growth in the affiliation movement had effectively halted and with the growth in the union movement throughout the decade, members of affiliated locals fell to between 1 and 2 per cent of the unionized work force.

Although the NDP did not introduce the idea of union affiliation, it did evince a resolve to make the affiliation movement successful. Except for the minor change which gave affiliated members the same rights at constituency meetings as individual party members,[18] the NDP adopted the affiliation formula used by the CCF. Immediately after its creation, the NDP began to work on strengthening its ties with labour in general and in rebuilding the affiliation movement in particular. For example, in the summer of 1962 an NDP-labour liaison committee recommended the declaration of a political month, whose purpose was: "(a) to keep trade union membership continuously aware of their political responsibilities; (b) to increase affiliated and individual memberships; and (c) to establish an identity of interests between trade unionists and the party."[19]

Various institutional arrangements were established to increase participation in the affiliation movement. Late in 1964 the CLC executive met with administrative personnel in the party at which time the group agreed to establish regular liaison through quarterly meetings. In addition, the CLC agreed to assist in persuading delinquent unions to bring their payments to the party up to date.[20] The key officer from the CLC side of the arrangement was the director of political education. An examination of party files shows that virtually every year the CLC's director of political education would mount a drive to increase the affiliation of trade unions with the party, usually by contacting the political education directors of national or international unions, who in turn would contact the union locals.[21] More generally and symbolically, the CLC executive committee continued to pass resolutions in favour of affiliation. Typical of these efforts was a 1969 resolution recommending "to all affiliated organizations that a special all-out effort be made in the next two years to increase substantially the affiliation to the NDP, and their [the locals] participation in the Canadian COPE program."[22] On the party side, the federal secretary assumed the major responsibility for increasing affiliation. As in the CLC, much of the communication between the federal secretary and the national or international unions was

TABLE 3
Unions Affiliated with the NDP and Membership of Affiliated Unions as a Percentage of Total Union Membership, Selected Years

Year	Number of Affiliated Locals	Members of Affiliated Locals ('000s)	Total Union Membership ('000s)	Union Members Affiliated (%)
1961	278	71	1423	5.0
1962	612	186	1449	12.9
1963	689	218	1493	14.6
1964	683	216	1589	13.6
1969	764	256	2075	12.3
1974	754	283	2732	10.4
1979	745	295	3397	8.7
1984	730	267	3651	7.3

Source: NDP files, "Organizatons affiliated with the NDP," selected years; Canada, Labour Canada, *Directory of Labour Organizations in Canada*, 1984.

through the latter's political action or political education coordinators.[23] The federal secretary also maintained close contact with party or union organizers and either directly or through the organizers established contact with union locals.[24]

Despite the prodigious effort on the part of the NDP and the CLC to increase affiliation, the affiliation movement did not grow appreciably. There was a change in the size of the affiliation movement after the transition from the CCF to the NDP, but the change was much more modest than originally anticipated. As table 3 illustrates, by 1962 over 600 locals with almost 200,000 members had affiliated to the party, accounting for 12.9 per cent of the unionized work force. In terms of the proportion of union members affiliated with the party, 1963 was the high water mark, when 14.6 per cent of unionized workers belonged to affiliated locals. Although this might appear to represent an encouraging increase in labour's support for the party less than three years after its founding, it should be borne in mind that only 29.8 per cent of non-agricultural paid workers were unionized in 1963.[25]

After 1963, the data indicate marginal changes in the number of union locals affiliated coupled with marginal increases in the absolute number of union members who belonged to affiliated

TABLE 4
*Organizations Affiliated to the NDP,
by Province, April 1985*

Province	Number of Affiliated Locals	Percentage of Affiliated Locals Nationwide	Number of Affiliated Members ('000s)	Percentage of Affiliated Members Nationwide
British Columbia	56	7.7	30.5	11.4
Alberta	20	2.7	5.7	2.1
Saskatchewan	33	4.5	10.5	3.9
Manitoba	42	5.8	12.0	4.5
Ontario	552	75.6	202.3	75.7
Quebec	12	1.6	2.9	1.1
New Brunswick	5	0.7	.6	0.2
Nova Scotia	7	1.0	2.3	0.8
Prince Edward Island	2	0.3	.5	0.2
Newfoundland	1	0.1	.05	0.0
TOTAL	730	100.0	267.35	99.9

Source: NDP files.

locals. More striking is the steady decline after 1963 in the proportion of union members affiliated with the party. By 1969 it had dropped to 12.3 per cent, and it continued to fall – to 10.4 per cent in 1974, 8.7 per cent in 1979, and finally to 7.3 per cent in 1984.

It is important not to overdraw the parallels between the experiences of the CCF and the NDP with the affiliation movement. By the 1950s the affiliation movement with the CCF was collapsing both relative to the overall growth in the union movement as well as in absolute terms from over 100 locals to less than 50. For the NDP, however, there has been an overall stabilization in the affiliation movement at approximately 750 locals, a level significantly below expectations in 1961, but nonetheless stable. The relative decline of the affiliation movement with the NDP is due to two facts: few locals which did not join in the years immediately after the party's creation have joined subsequently; and very few of the unions which have emerged since 1961 have decided to affiliate, an issue explored more fully in the next chapter.

To gain a fuller perspective on the potential political effect of union affiliation with the NDP, it is useful to examine the regional distribution of affiliated locals. The data in table 4 illustrate the significant regional strengths and weaknesses of union affiliation across the country. Of the 730 union locals affiliated in 1985, more than three-quarters (75.6 per cent) were located in Ontario. Most of the remaining affiliates were from the West (20.7 per cent). Less than 2 per cent of unions affiliated with the NDP in 1985 were Quebec-based locals, and slightly more than 2 per cent were from the Atlantic region. Nowhere in the country is union affiliation strong. East of the Ottawa River, it is almost non-existent.

CONCLUSION

In evaluating the linkage between organized labour and the NDP it becomes obvious that the party, like its organizational predecessor, the CCF, is not a labour party or a party controlled by organized labour. Rather it is a social democratic party with links of varying strength to the union movement, some of which are purposefully weak.

The personnel links can most readily be judged a success, in large part because the party's founders intended to provide only modest personnel overlap with organized labour. Unions are an important segment of the party, but the relationship between party and labour was so designed that labour's position would be clearly and distinctly a minority one. Furthermore, even within its minority role, labour tends to under-represent itself on party decision-making bodies.[26]

The financial contributions to the party from organized labour are important and substantial, but do not overshadow other sources. Affiliation fees constitute a minor proportion of party financing, largely because so few locals are affiliated. The other financial contributions from unions are highly variable; large and significant during election years and modest during non-election years. In comparison with the corporate financing of the Liberal and Progressive Conservative parties on a year-to-year basis, irrespective of whether an election is being held, union financial contributions have not enabled the NDP to compete on an equal footing.

The most disappointing linkage in the union-party relationship is the strength of the affiliation movement. Considerable efforts to increase affiliation have yielded few dividends. The substantial growth in affiliation that was expected in 1961 simply has not materialized. This failure is an important barometer of the ability of organized labour to deliver on its commitment to the party. It is not due to a lack of effort or commitment on the part of the union leadership, particularly within the CLC. Rather, it arises largely from the way in which the affiliation movement has been institutionalized, and from the logic that flows from that structure.

CHAPTER FOUR

Union-Party Affiliation as a Collective Action Problem

Why are so few union members affiliated with the New Democratic party? At the high point of the affiliation movement, slightly less than 15 per cent of union members belonged to affiliated locals; by 1984 this had declined to less than 8 per cent. Because less than 40 per cent of the non-agricultural paid work force was unionized that year, in fact only 2.8 per cent of the labour force belonged to NDP-affiliated union locals.

For many analysts, the failure of the affiliation movement can be explained by ideology.[1] One view is that liberal union members within a liberal political culture do not accept the idea of tying themselves organizationally to any party, and especially to a social democratic party.[2] Others suggest that the ideology of business unionism has been imposed on Canada's union leaders through their links with international, and especially American-based, unions.[3]

This study argues that the failure of the affiliation movement can be explained for the most part without reference to the ideology of Canadians in general or of union leaders in particular. The argument is founded on the structure of the rules of affiliation. That structure fragments the decision on union affiliation, allowing literally thousands of individual union locals to make their own choice based on self-interest utility maximization. One implication of such a structure is that union locals are encouraged to "free ride," rather than to pay the costs of affiliating with the party. A second implication is that even if a union, through its leaders and membership, has a pro-affiliation ideology, the balance of costs and benefits should still lead it to prefer not to affiliate. The issue of a union's ideology is therefore secondary.

A third implication is that changing the structure of the rules of affiliation may or may not increase the incidence of affiliation. It is very likely that some unions have an ideological predisposition against affiliating with the NDP. Our analysis suggests that many unions choose not to affiliate under the present rules even if they do not have such a predisposition. It is not possible at present to know how large each of these groups is, and rates of affiliation are not a good surrogate measure. Because the affiliation decision is made by union locals, and because there are well over 10,000 union locals in Canada, measuring the true ideological predisposition towards affiliation would be a formidable task, even if one attempted to estimate the population mean through a sampling procedure. The unavailability of such attitudinal survey data becomes moot, however, *if* it can be demonstrated that even unions ideologically predisposed to affiliation should not affiliate under the present rules. Before exploring this argument in depth, it is useful to examine another factor that has inhibited growth in the affiliation movement, namely, membership in a public sector union.

There were significant changes in the structure and composition of the Canadian union movement from 1966 to 1984; in particular, there was increased Canadianization, and a rapid growth in the unionization of the public sector. The catalyst for these developments was the passage of the Public Service Staff Relations Act (PSSRA) in 1967. This act provided for union certification (based on national organizations) for professionals and public servants and also for a combination of binding arbitration and the right to strike as mechanisms of conflict resolution. As a consequence of the passage of this act, large numbers of employees became eligible for collective bargaining, and it was within these groups that the highest rate of unionization occurred in subsequent years.[4]

Indeed, the passage of the PSSRA has had a very significant effect on both the size and shape of the union movement in Canada. In 1966, 30.7 per cent of non-agricultural paid workers were unionized, a figure which had remained remarkably stable since the end of the Second World War. In total, approximately 1.7 million Canadians were union members. By 1984, the number of union members had more than doubled to 3.7 million, increasing the percentage of non-agricultural paid workers which were unionized to 39.2 per cent (see table 5).

TABLE 5
Number of Unions and Membership, by Type of Union in Canada, 1966 and 1984

Type of Union	1966 Number	%	1984 Number	%
International	111	21.8	71	8.9
National	55	10.8	151	18.9
Other	344	67.4	577	72.2
TOTAL	510	100.0	799	100.0

	1966 Membership ('000s)	%	1984 Membership ('000s)	%
International	1220	70.2	1462	40.0
National	445	25.6	2050	56.1
Other	71	4.2	139	3.8
TOTAL	1736	100.0	3651	100.0

Source: Canada, Labour Canada, *Directory of Labour Organizations in Canada*, table A.

The data in table 5 also illustrate that most of the growth has taken place within national unions. In 1966, 70.2 per cent of union members belonged to Canadian branches of international unions; by 1984 this had declined to 40.0 per cent. Conversely, membership in national unions had increased from 0.4 million to 2.1 million, and in 1984 represented well over half of all union members. Unionization within the public sector accounts for much of the overall growth in union membership between 1966 and 1984. In 1966, only one of the six largest unions was a public sector union. By 1984, the three largest unions in Canada were all public sector ones and together accounted for 19.6 per cent of union members.[5]

Public sector unions differ from many other unions in Canada in several respects. For example, as Morley Gunderson notes, they are much more likely to be white-collar professionals or semi-professionals and to have different attitudes about their status:

The attitude of professional unions toward other unions, especially blue-collar workers, will probably continue to be one of aloofness, in spite of many of their common problems. Professional unions have no history of working class struggle; their members come from social backgrounds that are vastly different than most manual or even white-collar unionists; and, the occupational prestige of professionals rests on their being able to distinguish themselves as something apart from other workers. Rather than solidifying the labour movement by extending its influence to higher income and education groups, the unionization of professionals may well inject schisms, especially along political grounds.[6]

Perhaps even more importantly, insofar as union affiliation is concerned, government is the employer for public sector unionists. Because it is the employer, and because there is a strong potential for them to have adversarial roles in the collective bargaining process, it is not appropriate for these unions to affiliate themselves with any party, including the NDP. In light of this special political context, public sector unionists are excluded from the analysis of potential affiliates of the NDP.

This decision detracts little from the argument. It was noted in chapter 3 that affiliation with the NDP peaked by the late 1960s and has remained remarkably stable since that time. If public sector unionists are included in the total union membership, the conclusion would be that affiliation with the NDP has declined over time. If public sector unionists are excluded, the conclusion is that affiliation has remained stable and is static at rates far below those expected in 1961. In either case, the central question remains: why has affiliation remained so low?

CHOOSING TO AFFILIATE

The decision on affiliating with a political party presents unions with a binary choice: they can affiliate, or they can choose not to affiliate. Assume that individuals (and unions) are self-interested utility maximizers. Unions, in choosing whether to affiliate are assumed to ask: "What do we get in return for affiliating?" And: "What do we get if we choose not to affiliate?" The latter question is important because it highlights the fact that the goal of union affiliation – a stronger parliamentary party – has the characteristics of a collective good, in which individuals cannot be excluded from consumption once the good has been provided.

The problem of collective action arises when individuals are better off not contributing to the group because their contribution will change only marginally the amount of good provided to them, and hence they choose a "free ride." This problem arises when the group is large, or when there exists no subset of the group for whom the provision of the good outweighs the costs. One way in which this "group latency" may be overcome is through the use of selective incentives – individual rewards given to induce collective action.[7]

If the monetary cost of affiliating with the party is marginal,[8] the decision must turn on the benefits of affiliation. With the collective good defined as a high rate of union affiliation, decision-makers in unions are assumed to ask: "To what extent is the supply of that collective good increased by our affiliation?" For small unions, the answer is that the amount of good provided increases very little, and any costs should provide a sufficient deterrent to affiliation. For large unions, the decision to affiliate may have a marked effect on the amount of overall affiliation. Because they seek a high rate of affiliation, and because their affiliation has a significant effect on the amount of overall affiliation, they should choose to affiliate.

This simple model can explain the differential rates of union-party affiliation in Britain and Canada. The comparison with Britain is important for two reasons. First of all, many have argued that in aligning the NDP more closely with organized labour, the party adopted the model of the British Labour party. But, affiliation has been much less successful in Canada. If the British Labour party is the model, why is the outcome so different? Secondly, Britain is a good comparison because the pay-off structure with respect to affiliation is so different in the two countries. In Britain, national union bodies affiliate with the Labour party. In Canada, union locals affiliate with the NDP. Some national and international unions in Canada have hundreds and even thousands of locals, each of which decides individually on the matter of affiliation. The benefits which accrue through the affiliation of the larger bodies are much greater. In addition, the selective incentives for affiliation are different in the two countries. When affiliating with the Labour party, British unions receive a vote at the party conference for each affiliated individual. Canadian unions, however, receive a vote for each 1,000 members or major fraction thereof. In both instances, the rules in Britain are more likely to favour affiliation.

Parenthetically, the electoral success of the British Labour party and the relative electoral failure of the federal NDP does not diminish the logic of the analysis. The British comparison would be inappropriate only if rates of affiliation waxed and waned with the party's popularity, or if unions delayed affiliation until the party was successful at the polls. Such has not been the case in Britain. The affiliation movement was well under way before the Labour party was a serious contender for power. By 1901, only a year after the creation of the Labour Representation Committee (which changed its name to the Labour party in 1906), fully 22 per cent of union members belonged to affiliated unions, despite the party having only two of 670 members of parliament. By 1911, almost half (47.8 per cent) of British union members belonged to affiliated unions. This growth took place despite the Labour party receiving approximately 8 per cent of the votes and 6 per cent of the seats in the House of Commons in the two elections held in 1910. By the time the Labour party reached the status of official opposition in 1922, more than 50 per cent of union members belonged to affiliated unions.[9] Thus, in Britain the rules seem to have favoured affiliation even before the Labour party became an electoral success. In Canada the rules favoured non-affiliation even if the party were to become successful at the polls.

COLLECTIVE ACTION IN BRITAIN AND CANADA

Before proceeding with the data analysis, recall the assumption that unions have as their goal a high rate of affiliation with the party. It would be misleading to assume that all unions in either Britain or Canada desire a strong labour party. Rather, it is the major union centrals in the two countries which have this goal. It was the Trades Union Congress (TUC), not "organized labour," which was responsible for defining the relationship between the unions and the party in Britain. Similarly, it was the Canadian Labour Congress, not "organized labour," which led the movement to transform the CCF into the NDP, complete with provisions for affiliation. Therefore, it is useful to define the group which

TABLE 6
British Trade Unions Affiliated with the TUC, by Size of Union, 1976

Size	Total Unions*	Unions Affiliated with TUC*	% Unions Affiliated with TUC
0–999	250 (0.6)	17 (0.1)	6.8
1,000–9,999	133 (3.6)	29 (1.0)	21.8
10,000–49,999	40 (8.2)	29 (6.8)	72.5
50,000–99,999	14 (8.1)	13 (8.3)	92.9
100,000+	25 (79.5)	25 (83.8)	100.0
TOTAL	462	113	24.5
Total Members	12,376,000	11,036,326	89.2

* Figures in Parentheses are percentage of union members in each category.
Source: Great Britain, *Department of Employment Gazette*, November 1977, 1203–05; Trades Union Congress, *Annual Report: Statistical Statement*, 1976, 675–715.

pursues union-party affiliation as the unions affiliated with the TUC in Britain and with the CLC in Canada.

On the surface, the British trade union movement appears to be extremely fragmented organizationally. In 1976 the approximately 12.4 million union members were distributed among 462 unions (table 6). However, most of the unions were relatively small; 383 (83 per cent) had fewer than 10,000 members each and together they constituted only 4.2 per cent of the organized work force. At the other extreme there were 25 unions, each with more than 100,000 members, and together representing almost 80 per cent of total union membership. In addition, 39 unions (8 per cent) had more than 50,000 members. Thus, although British workers were organized into a large number of unions, the great majority belonged to a relatively small number of large unions.

Only a minority of British unions affiliate with the TUC; in 1976, 113 of the 462 British unions were affiliated with the Congress and in 1980, 109 of 438 unions were TUC affiliates. However, as table 6 illustrates, the Congress has been very successful in affiliating the largest unions. Every one of the 25 unions with more than 100,000 members and all but one of the 39 with more than 50,000 members were affiliated with the TUC in 1976. Among the

TABLE 7
*TUC Unions Affiliated with the British Labour Party,
by Size of Union, 1976*

Size	Unions Affiliated with TUC*	TUC Unions Affiliated with Labour party*	% TUC Unions Affiliated with party
0–999	17 (0.1)	2 (0.0)	11.8
1,000–9,999	29 (1.0)	13 (0.7)	44.8
10,000–49,999	29 (6.8)	14 (4.6)	48.3
50,000–99,999	13 (8.3)	8 (6.1)	61.5
100,000+	25 (83.8)	20 (88.6)	80.0
TOTAL	113	57	50.4
			81.0
Total Members	11,036,326	8,926,326	

Source: Minkin, *The Labour Party Conference*, appendix 3, 353–5.

smaller unions, however, the TUC's lack of success has been almost as complete as its success among the larger unions. Thus, of the 250 unions with fewer than 1,000 members, only 17 (6.8 per cent) were affiliated with the TUC. In sum, although the TUC affiliates slightly less than 25 per cent of all British unions, these unions together comprise over 11 million members, or 87 per cent of organized workers in Britain.

With respect to affiliation with the Labour party, the data in table 7 reveal that of the 113 unions affiliated with the TUC in 1976, only 57 (50.4 per cent) were affiliated with the Labour party. However, the affiliated unions had approximately 8.9 million members, representing 81 per cent of TUC membership. Upon closer inspection, the data illustrate that of the 25 unions with more than 100,000 members in 1976, fully 80 per cent (20) were affiliated with the party. Conversely, only 2 of 17 (11.8 per cent) TUC unions with fewer than 1,000 members were affiliated with the party. Thus, the data indicate a strong relationship between union size and TUC membership, and a strong relationship between the size of TUC unions and affiliation with the Labour party ($r = .43$).

Recall that the rational-choice model posits that each actor (union) engages in a cost-benefit calculation with respect to affiliation. Because a high rate of union affiliation with the Labour party is the means to a collective good (by definition), any union in the group (that is, TUC affiliates) cannot be excluded from the benefits of its provision. Therefore, the value any union receives from affiliation equals the total amount received after affiliation minus the amount it would receive if it were a "free rider."

It is very difficult to estimate with any degree of certainty the point at which benefits exceed costs, because the benefits are not directly translatable into a cash value. By way of illustration, suppose that country *A* has five unions which together organize all of its 10 million union members. Suppose further that these unions agreed, through a central labour organization, to affiliate with a labour party. If one of the unions had 92 per cent of unionists, and the remaining 4 unions each had 2 per cent, we could reasonably conclude that the largest union would affiliate, provided costs were relatively low, because affiliation would produce almost total group affiliation. The remaining four unions, however, should choose not to affiliate because their affiliation would make very little difference, relatively, to the amount of the collective good they receive. From the example, it could be concluded that organized labour was a privileged group and that its organizational structure encouraged the smaller unions to be free riders. Labour can achieve its collective good, but at suboptimal rates of affiliation.

In contrast, suppose country *B*'s 10 million unionists were divided among 10,000 unions, each with 1,000 members. Because any union's affiliation would constitute only .01 per cent of the total affiliation, the costs incurred probably would preclude each union from affiliating. Although, once again, the value derived from affiliation cannot be compared in cash value to the affiliation dues, nonetheless it is reasonable to conclude that each union's affiliation would not make a significant difference in the amount of the collective good received.

Britain falls somewhere between these two extreme examples. Even though a relatively small number of unions organize a majority of unionists, no single union is able to supply a majority of the collective good. This does not mean, of course, that it is necessarily irrational for any union to affiliate. The amount of the good received as a result of affiliation simply has to exceed the cost. However, because the former cannot be derived deductively, it must be estimated inductively. A reasonable estimate

TABLE 8
*Representation at
Labour Party Conference, 1976*

Organization	Delegates	Number	Votes	% of Votes
Trade Unions	587	54	5,669,000	88.7
Socialist Societies	10	8	31,000	0.5
Co-operative Organizations	4	1	19,000	0.3
Constituency Labour Parties	552	548	673,000	10.5
TOTAL	1,153	611	6,392,000	100.0

Source: Labour Party of Great Britain, *Report of the Annual Conference*, 1976, 125.

may be approximately 10 per cent of the group. In the British case, 10 per cent of the group translates into approximately one million unionists. Although this number may appear to be a rather low estimate of the proportion of the group which can contribute a significant difference, nonetheless the inclusion of an additional million unionists affiliated with the Labour party as a result of one union's action seems to make an appreciable difference. In 1976, three British unions were above or approached this cut-off point and each was affiliated with the Labour party.

The Labour party also provides unions with a selective incentive to affiliate in the form of votes at the party's conference. Unions which affiliate with the party are assigned one conference vote for each member. As table 8 indicates, this has led to union domination of the party conferences. Of the 6.4 million votes at the 1976 Labour party conference, fully 5.7 million (88.7 per cent) were cast in blocks by unions.

It is obvious that this method of allocating selective incentives also favours large unions over smaller unions, because the former receive a much larger share of party conference votes than the latter. However, if one assumes that a union weighs the benefits of its conference votes not against the total conference vote but against non-union votes, then the point of reference for unions is the combined non-union vote, which, in 1976, was slightly

TABLE 9
*Canadian Unions Affiliated with the CLC,
by Type of Union, 1984*

Union Type	Total Unions	Unions Affiliated with CLC	% Unions Affiliated with CLC
National and International	222	75	33.8
Other	577	66	11.4
TOTAL	799	141	17.6
Total Members	3,651,000	2,050,000	56.1

Source: Canada, Labour Canada, *Directory of Labour Organization in Canada*, 1984, table 4.

more than 700,000. Again, however, it is difficult to estimate the point at which the benefits to be derived from a union's conference votes will outweigh the costs of affiliation. In the British case, the cut-off point appears to be approximately 35,000 union members, or about 5 per cent of non-union conference votes. Of the 44 unions with more than 35,000 members, 33 (75 per cent) were affiliated with the Labour party. In contrast, only 24 (35 per cent) of the 69 TUC unions below that threshold were affiliated. Overall, on the basis of size alone – and assuming a cost-benefit calculation on the part of individual unions – this could explain the behaviour of 69 per cent of the unions. In sum, TUC unions appear to be a privileged group with respect to party affiliation because of their relative size and the system of selective incentives offered to them.

The Canadian labour movement is even more fragmented than its British counterpart. As table 9 illustrates, in 1984 there were 799 unions which organized 3.7 million Canadians. The vast majority (96 per cent) of unionists belonged to one of the 222 national or international federated unions, and the remaining 4 per cent to one of the 577 directly chartered or independent locals. As in the British case, there is a small number of relatively large unions and a large number of small unions. For example, the six largest unions in 1984 included almost one-third (30.5 per cent) of all union members. Like the TUC, the CLC has been only moderately successful in affiliating unions. Of the 799 unions in Canada in

1984, only 141 (17.6 per cent) were affiliated with the CLC. Members of the CLC included 75 national or international unions and 66 directly chartered locals, whose total membership of 2.1 million constituted 56.1 per cent of the organized work force. As with the TUC, a disproportionate share of the CLC membership belongs to large unions. For example, in 1984, its six largest affiliates accounted for approximately 1.1 million members (54.4 per cent of total affiliated members).

The major difference between the British and Canadian cases with respect to union-party affiliation is the organizational level at which unions affiliate with the party. The rule that affiliation is at the level of union local in Canada had the effect of transforming the CLC's 141 affiliates in 1984 into 8,744 individual units which must decide on affiliation with the party (see table 10). Slightly more than half of the CLC unions are in the public sector. Eliminating them reduces the number of union locals deciding on affiliation to 4,169. As one might expect, these union locals are relatively small, ranging from as few as 4 members to as many as 12,000, with a mean size of 234 members.

Recall that individuals are assumed to calculate the benefits of affiliation based on the incremental increase that accompanies their decision for affiliation less that which they would receive from the "non-excludable" good were they not to affiliate. Again, it is difficult to estimate the size at which benefits exceed costs. If one applied to Canada the cut-off which was applied to the British data (10 per cent of total group), then there would be no individual unions for whom affiliation would be rational. The ratio would need to be reduced by a factor of ten, to 1 per cent of group size, for there to be any affiliations from among utility-maximizing unions. The pay-off at the 1 per cent level is sufficiently small that the selective incentive would appear not to produce any contributions towards collective action. Thus, with respect to affiliation with the NDP, CLC union locals appear to be a good example of a latent group.

Do selective incentives, in the form of individual rewards, assist Canadian union locals to overcome their latency? The data in table 11 suggest that the answer is a categorical "no". In contrast to the provision of one conference vote per member of affiliated unions in Britain, the NDP allots one convention delegate for each 1,000 members or major fraction thereof. Thus, a large local would have from 10 to 12 votes at the party's convention. This

TABLE 10
CLC Unions Affiliated with the NDP,
by Type of Union, 1984

Union Type	Unions Affiliated with CLC	Union Locals Affiliated with CLC	Non-Public-Sector Union Locals Affiliated with CLC	Non-Public-Sector CLC Union Locals Affiliated with NDP	% Non-Public-Sector CLC Locals Affiliated with NDP
National and International	75	8,678	4,103	702	17.1
Other	66	66	66	28*	–
TOTAL	141	8,744	4,169	730	17.5
Total Members	2,050,000	2,050,000	1,285,813	267,348	20.8

* Includes local unions and unions not affiliated with the CLC.

Source: Canada, Labour Canada, *Directory of Labour Organization in Canada*, 1984; NDP files.

TABLE 11
Representation at NDP Convention, 1981

Organization	Accredited Delegates	% of Total Delegates
Affiliated Unions	864	29.9
Central Labour	195	6.8
NDP Federal Council	135	4.7
NDP Federal Caucus	28	0.9
Constituency Party	1,646	57.0
Young New Democrats	20	0.7
TOTAL	2,888	100.0

Source: NDP files, Report of the Credentials Committee, NDP convention, 1981.

corresponds to approximately 0.6 per cent of non-union accredited delegates at the NDP's 1981 convention, less (by approximately a factor of 10) than the proportion estimated to produce rational affiliation in Britain. The small increment which each union local can contribute to the collective good, when coupled with the small selective incentive awarded to induce cooperation, produces the expectation of very low rates of affiliation with the NDP.

The data in table 10 strongly support this expectation. Of the 4,169 private sector union locals affiliated with the CLC in 1984, 730 (17.5 per cent) were affiliated with the NDP. The remaining 82.5 per cent of CLC private sector union locals had decided against affiliating with the NDP. From a utility-maximizing perspective, the latter unions are behaving in an eminently rational fashion. Because there are so many union locals, and because individually they are so small, affiliation by any given union local will not result in a significant increase in the total amount of affiliation. For example, if a very large union local with 10,000 members chose to affiliate, it would increase the total number of affiliated private sector CLC union members from the current 20.8 per cent to 21.6 per cent, hardly a significant increase. It also would increase the rate of NDP affiliation among all Canadian unionists from 7.3 per cent to 7.6 per cent. More important, perhaps, that same union would receive ten convention delegates, out of a total of almost 2,900 delegates, over 1,800 of whom are non-union delegates. With such a small pay-off for affiliation, it is not surprising that so few unions have chosen to affiliate.

CONCLUSION

Among the many insights of the public choice approach to political behaviour, and especially group behaviour, is the highlighting of the contrast between the group interest and the interests of individual members of groups in pursuing collective action. Although a group may define a collective goal for itself, and although every member of the group may agree that the goal is worth pursuing collectively, individual group members may have an incentive to let others pay while they have a free ride.

The public choice approach provides some very useful insights into the question of union affiliation with the NDP. The rules on affiliation make decision-making so fragmented, and the number of union locals is so large, that simply maintaining contact with all locals, let alone lending support to encourage affiliation, becomes a herculean effort. Even among the large industrial unions like the Steelworkers and Auto Workers, which have been among the most committed to political action since the 1940s, fewer than half their locals were affiliated with the NDP in 1984. Although the leadership of these unions has paid much lip service to the need for political action and political affiliation, and despite the significant efforts that have been expended in support of the CCF and the NDP, most of their locals still find it is not in their self-interest to affiliate.

For those unions which do affiliate – in 1984 there were 730 – the conclusion is that the assumption about their decision being based on self-interested utility maximization was wrong. They chose to affiliate even though their decision affected only marginally the amount of the collective good provided. However, more than 4 out of 5 locals acted in a way consistent with the expectations from the self-interested utility-maximizing assumption, and in doing so ensured the failure of the affiliation movement.

CHAPTER FIVE

Electoral Consequences of Union Affiliation

What effect does a union local's affiliation with the NDP have on the political attitudes and behaviour of Canadian voters with union links? If members of affiliated unions are not more likely to identify with and vote for the NDP, and if they are not more likely to have attitudes consistent with the New Democratic philosophy, then the issue of the level of union affiliation with the party is moot. Conversely, if membership in an affiliated local has the effect of aligning individuals more closely with the NDP, the overall importance of affiliation is enhanced. This chapter examines the extent to which union affiliation with the NDP affects the political attitudes and behaviour of individuals.

To date, very little empirical research has been conducted on the union basis of partisan support. For example, none of the major reports of the Canadian national election studies even mentions unions in its analysis.[1] In the few studies which have examined the effect of union membership on voting in Canada, no distinction is made between individuals belonging to unions affiliated with the NDP and those in unions not so affiliated. The assumption appears to be that all Canadian unionists should be equally inclined to support the party. For example, Miller presents data which show that twice as many union members voted for the NDP in 1968 (28 versus 14 per cent) as non-unionists, a marginal increase over the 1963 figures of 21 and 11 per cent respectively.[2] Chi and Perlin suggest that in 1968, 30.9 per cent of union members compared to 11.6 per cent of non-unionists voted for the NDP.[3] For 1965, their corresponding figures are 26.9 per cent and 14.9 per cent. Similarly, in a 1971 study of the determinants of party preference among manual workers in four

Ontario communities, Keddie found that 35 per cent of those who were union members were "consistent" NDP supporters whereas only 9 per cent of non-unionists consistently supported the NDP.[4]

The calculation of the percentage vote for the NDP among union and non-union groups is affected by a number of decisions made when operationalizing the variables. For example, is the sample weighted to adjust for regional oversampling or not? If a community rather than the national electorate is sampled, are the effects of living in that community taken into account? As well, the researcher must decide whether the percentages are to be based on marginal totals that include non-voters and refusals, or whether the latter are filtered out. In addition to all of these questions, for which there is no single correct strategy, one must decide whether union members are to be defined simply as those who are themselves members of a union, or whether those whose immediate family includes a union member are to be included.

The decision on each of these questions will affect the percentage of New Democratic voters that will be found among groups of union members and non-unionists. The point can be illustrated from the 1979 national election study. For 1979, using a weighted national sample, and including non-voters and those who refuse to answer in the analysis, 22.2 per cent of union members voted NDP compared with 11.9 per cent of non-unionist voters.

Because there is much evidence to suggest that the adult political socialization which takes place occurs mainly within a family unit, members of union families should be more likely to vote NDP, although at rates below those for union members.[5] The 1979 data confirm both of these expectations. Among members of families with a union member, 19.9 per cent voted NDP compared with 10.2 per cent of those with no union members in their families. If those who did not vote or who refused to report their vote to the interviewer are excluded, the data show a greater proportion of each group voting NDP – that is, the number of NDP voters in each group will remain the same, but the marginal totals will be reduced. Consistent with these expectations, 24.1 per cent of union members who voted, voted NDP compared with 13.1 per cent of non-unionists. Among those with a union member in their immediate family, 21.5 per cent voted NDP compared with 11.3 per cent of voters with no union member in their family. Furthermore, these data are remarkably consistent with those from the 1984 election study (data not shown).

These 1979 data illustrated several important points. First, using any operational definition, union members were twice as likely to vote NDP as voters who are not members of unions. The effect of union membership appears to be to increase support for the NDP from about 10 to 12 per cent to approximately 20 to 24 per cent. None of the operational definitions resulted in NDP support among union members exceeding 25 per cent in any study of elections between 1968 and 1984. Second, the pattern of difference between union members and non-unionists was remarkably consistent whether union membership was defined narrowly – only those who themselves belong to a union – or, more broadly, to include those with a union member in their immediate family. To the extent that unions convey a political cue, the data suggest that the cue has relatively equal force upon the individual and his or her family. Third, in an absolute sense, the effect of the union cue is somewhat stronger among union members than among their family members, although not overwhelmingly so. When the analysis is based on union members alone, the observed effect of this variable is stronger than when the analysis focuses on union families. This last issue is important to the present analysis because of the way in which the union variable is used, and the way it is measured in the election studies. However, more on that below.

The analysis in this chapter and the next differs from conventional studies of the support of union members for the NDP because it distinguishes between members of those unions that are affiliated with the NDP and members of those that are not. It has been documented widely that trade union support is a prerequisite to the development of a strong social democratic political party.[6] Chapter 3 noted that organized labour has provided the NDP with personnel and financial support and also with the more symbolic support associated with union affiliation. It was hypothesized that a union's affiliation with the NDP acts as a cue to its members and represents an unambiguous attempt to influence both their political attitudes and their behaviour.[7] Whether or not members of affiliated unions respond to this cue is, of course, an empirical question.

To what extent will the effect of that cue be confined to members of unions themselves, and to what extent might it impinge on the attitudes and behaviour of family members? There are both theoretical and empirical reasons to expect that one should observe an effect among family members, although to a somewhat lesser extent than among union members.

On the theoretical front, it has become clear that socialization is a process that continues throughout life, and the family remains one of the primary socializing agents.[8] The influences that touch on each of us individually – such as political messages – are spread, at least potentially and by very significant socializing agents, to those who share our home. It is to be expected that some of the force of the cue will be lost through this secondary transmission of information – in some homes there may be very little dialogue about and exchange of political information – but it should be present and measurable nonetheless.

On a more empirical note, the 1979 data on the political effect of union membership illustrated an example of this process of family socialization at work. Members of union families proved more likely to vote NDP than members of non-union families by a factor of 2 to 1, a finding that corresponded almost exactly with the result when only union members were examined. That is, despite union members being somewhat more likely to vote NDP than members of union families, the measured effect of either variable in relation to its non-unionist or non-unionist family counterpart is the same.

A third reason for using union families instead of union members relates to the number of cases. Data from national election studies will be used to examine the potentially important mobilizing effect of union affiliation with the NDP on levels of individual support for the party. However, in 1984 less than 3 per cent of the organized work force belonged to union locals affiliated with the party. Sampling theory suggests that when using quasi-random techniques on a group which makes up a very small proportion of the population, very few members of that group will be found in a sample the size of those used in national election studies. The use of union families provides an increase in the number of individuals who are affected by union affiliation. An expansion of the relevant group is crucial in facilitating the application of statistical controls to account for potentially confounding effects. Unfortunately, the data sets do not allow the expansion of the definition of union members to union families in both the 1979 and 1984 studies. Although the 1979 national election study asked union members and members of families which included a union member to identify the union, the 1984 national election study asked this question only of union members. That is, although respondents in 1984 were asked whether a family member belonged to a union, they were not asked which union that was. Consequently, it is not possible to determine whether the union was affiliated with the NDP.

A virtue can be made of this necessity by structuring the analysis to employ "hard" and "soft" measures of union affiliation. For the 1979 portion of the analysis, the union affiliation variable is based on those who are themselves union members or have a family member who is a union member. For 1984, it includes only those who are union members. The expectation was that the trends in the data would be the same with either measure, although the absolute differences likely will be greatest when only union members are used. However, given the very small number of cases available when only union members are used, the analysis using the 1984 data is much less detailed, and it was not possible to employ as many statistical controls. Rather than standing on their own, the analyses of the 1984 data should be seen as testing through replication the findings using the 1979 data.

MEASURES AND METHODS

Using data from the 1979 and 1984 Canadian national election studies and from the files of the NDP,[9] the extent to which a union's affiliation with the NDP affects both the political attitudes and behaviour of its members was examined. The expectation was that members of union locals affiliated with the NDP would exhibit attitudinal and behavioural characteristics which differ from those of both non-unionists and members of union locals not affiliated with the NDP. Specifically, the hypothesis was that union status acts as an important independent variable affecting an individual's class awareness and ideological self-image; his/her perception of the NDP and its leader and local candidates; the direction of party identification; perceptions of issues; and, ultimately, vote. In short, union status has both a direct effect on vote and an indirect effect, acting through variables which previous research has shown to be important determinants of voting.[10]

Because the union status variable is very important to this analysis, a detailed discussion of the manner in which it was generated is warranted. Union status has been operationally defined as a trichotomous variable, including (1) non-unionists; (2)

members of union locals not affiliated with the NDP; and (3) members of NDP-affiliated union locals. For the 1979 data, an individual is considered to be a union member if he, personally, or a family member, belongs to a union. Similarly, a member of an NDP-affiliated union is one who personally belongs to an affiliated local or is part of a family, one of whose members belongs to an affiliated local. For the 1984 analysis, the affiliation status of respondents in union families could not be determined, and the analysis was therefore confined to union members.

Both election studies included information on individuals' union affiliation and, for 1979, family members' affiliation. In those cases in which the union was not specified (such as "other international union"), the original interview schedules were examined to obtain the name of the union.[11] Unfortunately, respondents were not specifically asked for the union local to which they belonged and thus most did not supply that information. In those cases, determination of whether an individual belonged to an NDP-affiliated local was made in the following manner. First, party files were examined to determine whether any locals of the individual's union were affiliated with the NDP in the respondent's province. If not, he was deemed a member of a non-affiliated local. If there were locals of that union affiliated with the NDP in the province, the procedure was repeated for the individual's constituency. For example, if an individual belonged to the UAW and lived in the constituency of Windsor-Walkerville, and if it was determined that a UAW local in Windsor was affiliated with the party in 1979 or 1984, as the case may be, that individual was coded a member of an affiliated local. The distribution of locals affiliated with the NDP – over two-thirds are in Ontario and they tend to cluster in the larger urban areas – makes this procedure less tentative than it might initially appear. The distribution of cases on this variable is very much in keeping with expectations based on aggregate data. However, because the union could not be identified for those with union members in the family in 1984, the proportion of members of affiliated unions in the 1984 sample (2 per cent) is substantially below that in the 1979 study (5 per cent).

DATA ANALYSIS

Table 12 examines the effect of union affiliation with the NDP on levels of identification with and vote for the Liberal, Progressive

TABLE 12
*Party Identification and Vote,
by Union Status, 1979**

	Non-Unionists (%)	Members of Non-affiliated Unions (%)	Members of Affiliated Unions (%)	N
A. Party Identification			
Liberal	44.8	45.2	39.8	(1076)
Conservative	34.9	23.2	22.5	(719)
New Democrat	9.5	17.5	32.6	(331)
N	(1376)	(908)	(127)	
B. Vote			
Liberal	42.2	41.8	40.4	(899)
Conservative	43.1	31.9	28.6	(817)
New Democrat	11.5	20.0	29.9	(336)
N	(1221)	(812)	(110)	

* Columns do not sum to 100 because "other" parties are included in the analysis but excluded from the table. Non-identifiers and non-voters are excluded.

Conservative, and New Democratic parties in 1979. The data suggest that union-party affiliation has a moderately positive effect on rates of support for the NDP. For instance, in 1979, 32.6 per cent of members of NDP-affiliated locals identified with the NDP compared with 17.5 per cent of members of non–NDP-affiliated unions and 9.5 per cent of non-unionists, respectively (see panel A). Data on reported vote in 1979 (panel B) reveal similar patterns. For example, nearly 30 per cent of union members belonging to NDP-affiliated locals reported voting for the NDP in 1979 compared with 20 per cent of unionists whose locals were not affiliated with the party. The corresponding figure for non-unionists was 11.5 per cent. Recalling our earlier analysis which found that in 1979, 22.8 per cent of all unionists voted for the NDP, the decision of union locals to affiliate with the party appears to produce a significant increase in party support.

The finding that in 1979 support for the Liberal party was greater than for the NDP even among members of NDP-affiliated locals is also important for an understanding of Canadian politics. Nearly 40 per cent of the latter identified with the Liberal party compared with 32.6 per cent who identified with the NDP. However, the difference between rates of identification with the Liberal and New Democratic parties is substantially less among

TABLE 13
*Party Identification and Vote,
by Union Status, 1984**

	Non-Unionists (%)	Members of Non-affiliated Unions (%)	Members of Affiliated Unions (%)	N
	A. Party Identification			
Liberal	35.4	35.4	20.7	(996)
Conservative	50.5	42.0	39.7	(1332)
New Democrat	13.1	21.0	39.7	(472)
N	(1697)	(1078)	(58)	
	B. Vote			
Liberal	25.9	24.9	7.5	(742)
Conservative	60.2	53.5	53.7	(1697)
New Democrat	13.1	20.3	38.8	(485)
N	(1761)	(1122)	(67)	

* Columns do not sum to 100 because "other" parties are included in the analysis but excluded from the table. Non-identifiers and non-voters are excluded.

members of affiliated locals (7.2 per cent) than among members of non-affiliated locals (27.7 per cent). Affiliation with the party may thus provide an important cue to the union rank and file. Nonetheless, the NDP's lack of electoral success can be attributed in part to the inability of union locals either to deliver more votes to the party or to stimulate higher rates of affiliation with the party.

The finding that union affiliation appears to have an important mobilizational effect on support for the NDP among union members is confirmed by data from the 1984 election study (table 13). Approximately 13 per cent of non-unionists identified with the NDP in 1984. This percentage almost doubled, to 21, among members of unaffiliated unions. Among members of union locals affiliated with the NDP, almost 40 per cent identified with the party. Once again there is a similar trend when the dependent variable is the party voted for, with the percentage increasing from 13 to 20 to 39 per cent for the three union status groups. As expected, the contrast among the groups is sharpened when only union members are included, although the number of cases becomes dangerously low.

The findings on NDP support among the union status groups are remarkable for their stability within a changing political climate and provide a useful illustration of several characteristics of Canadian political behaviour. First of all, the data in tables 12 and 13 illustrate the remarkable volatility of the Canadian electorate over a very brief period of time. In 1979, even among members of NDP-affiliated unions, more individuals voted for the Liberals than for any other party. By 1984, support for the Liberal party among this group had declined to less than 10 per cent. Conversely, the Conservatives moved from the least favoured to the most favoured party among this group over just five years. In describing and understanding the nature of the Canadian electorate, that volatility must be given its due.

Second, the data illustrate how significant social cleavages, when acted upon, can provide an important grounding for political attitudes and behaviour.[12] The stability in the pattern of NDP voting among the three union status groups suggests that the effects of union membership and union affiliation were able to withstand the force of a changing political tide. One might expect that such a factor would impinge upon other political attitudes and orientations.

A third factor which the data in tables 12 and 13 make evident is the boundary or limit of the mobilizational capacity of union affiliation. Quite clearly, this factor alone cannot win elections for the NDP. Even among members of affiliated unions, the NDP finished as the second choice in both 1979 and 1984. Simply put, many unionists ignore the political cue from their union, just as many Catholics or Protestants may ignore a political cue from their church. That said, it is worth reiterating that union affiliation with the NDP does exert an unmistakable influence by narrowing the gap between the NDP and its political opponents.

Historically, union support for the CCF/NDP has come disproportionately from industrial unions, especially from the United Automobile Workers (UAW) and the United Steelworkers of America (USWA). Indeed, 71 of the 127 members (56 per cent) of affiliated locals in the 1979 sample belonged to one of these unions.[13] Thus, one might argue that the conclusions on effects of affiliation drawn from the data in tables 12 and 13 are spurious; that the real causal factor is industrial as opposed to craft unionism. To test this hypothesis, UAW and USWA members were isolated to examine whether union local affiliation with the NDP is positively related to support for the NDP among otherwise similar individuals. The findings, presented in table 14, only partly sup-

TABLE 14
Party Identification and Vote,
by Union Status,
UAW-USWA *vs* Non–UAW–USWA, *1979**

	Liberal %	Conservative %	NDP %	N
A. Party Identification				
Member of Non-Affiliated Union				
UAW-USWA	48.6	23.9	15.7	(19)
non–UAW-USWA	45.1	23.2	17.5	(889)
Member of Affiliated Union				
UAW-USWA	34.2	28.0	34.2	(51)
non–UAW-USWA	44.7	19.7	31.6	(76)
B. Vote				
Member of Non-Affiliated Union				
UAW-USWA	41.8	30.5	27.7	(17)
non–UAW-USWA	41.8	31.9	19.7	(795)
Member of Affiliated Union				
UAW-USWA	34.6	30.3	35.1	(43)
non–UAW-USWA	43.3	26.9	26.9	(67)

* Row percentages

port the hypothesis. For example, panel A indicates very little difference in levels of identification with the NDP between UAW-USWA unionists and members of other unions. In each case, members of affiliated locals were approximately twice as likely as their non-affiliated counterparts to identify with the NDP. With respect to voting intention, however, the data in panel B indicate that UAW-USWA unionists were more likely to vote for the NDP than members of other unions. This trend is consistent for members of both non–NDP-affiliated and affiliated unions. It is also important to note that for each group of unionists, members of affiliated locals were more likely than members of non-affiliated unions to vote for the NDP.

One explanation for the stronger likelihood that UAW-USWA members will vote for the NDP is that these unions are located in constituencies in which the party is relatively strong. For example, the steel- and automobile-producing centres of Hamilton, Oshawa, and Windsor in Ontario have been bastions of NDP support. In such areas, an NDP vote is less likely to be seen as a wasted vote than in areas of NDP weakness. To test this hypothesis, a measure of the relative constituency strength of the NDP was included as a contextual variable. The results of the analysis including an additional control for region residence, are presented in table 15.

Three features of this analysis warrant specific comment. First, the distribution of members of NDP-affiliated union locals is very uneven across the regions. In Quebec and the Atlantic provinces, for example, the number of members of locals affiliated with the NDP in the 1979 sample is 4. The corresponding figures for Ontario and the West are 87 and 28, respectively.[14] These figures approximate the distribution of members of affiliated locals in the Canadian population, where in 1979 the proportion of affiliated union members by region was 4.6, 76, and 19.4 per cent for Quebec-Atlantic, Ontario, and the West, respectively.[15]

Second, the data illustrate a perceptible relationship between the constituency support for the party and the rate at which members of all groups support the party. For example, in Ontario, 6.6 per cent of non-unionists who lived in constituencies in which the NDP did very poorly in 1979 (0–15 per cent of the vote) identified with the party as compared with 13.9 per cent of their counterparts residing in constituencies where the NDP did substantially better (15.1–25 per cent of the vote) and 15.2 per cent of non-unionists in constituencies in which the NDP polled very well (over 25 per cent).

Third, and most important for the thesis advanced here, in each instance where there was more than a handful of cases, members of affiliated union locals identified with the NDP at higher levels than did members of non–NDP-affiliated unions. For instance, in Ontario constituencies in which the NDP received 15 to 25 per cent of the vote in 1979, 26.9 per cent of members of affiliated union locals identified with the NDP, compared with 21.4 per cent and 13.9 per cent for members of non–NDP-affiliated and non-unionists, respectively. Likewise, 41 per cent of NDP-affiliated union members in Ontario constituencies in which the NDP was very strong identified with the party, almost twice the rate of union members whose locals were not affiliated with the NDP (22.6 per cent). A similar pattern can be discerned among residents of the four western provinces. In constituencies in which the NDP was strong, members of NDP-affiliated locals are more likely to identify with the party (48.9 per cent) than either those in non–NDP-affiliated unions (38 per cent) or non-unionists (19.3 per cent).

TABLE 15
*Percentage NDP Identification and Vote,
by Union Status, Controlling for
Region and Level of Constituency Support for the NDP**

	Atlantic and Quebec		Ontario		West	
NDP Constituency Support	%	N	%	N	%	N

A. NDP Identification

NDP polled 0–15%						
Non-Union	5.1	(388)	6.6	(15)	4.9	(144)
Non-Affiliated Union	8.5	(317)	10.3	(60)	4.7	(47)
Affiliated Union	0	(3)	0	(4)	0	(0)
NDP polled 15.1–25%						
Non-Union	2.2	(71)	13.9	(208)	14.6	(73)
Non-Affiliated Union	19.1	(64)	21.4	(99)	17.5	(48)
Affiliated Union	0	(0)	26.9	(32)	0	(7)
NDP polled over 25%						
Non-Union	10.5	(10)	15.2	(134)	19.3	(155)
Non-Affiliated Union	3.9	(13)	22.6	(90)	38.0	(139)
Affiliated Union	0	(1)	41.0	(51)	48.9	(21)

B. NDP Vote

NDP polled 0–15%						
Non-Union	4.2	(341)	7.2	(138)	5.2	(116)
Non-Affiliated Union	8.7	(282)	15.0	(53)	5.1	(43)
Affiliated Union	0	(3)	0	(2)	0	(0)
NDP polled 15.1–25%						
Non-Union	4.5	(58)	16.3	(189)	22.4	(65)
Non-Affiliated Union	21.2	(55)	18.5	(94)	19.5	(43)
Affiliated Union	0	(0)	24.0	(31)	0	(5)
NDP polled over 25%						
Non-Union	33.3	(8)	22.3	(125)	21.6	(143)
Non-Affiliated Union	19.1	(11)	29.6	(79)	46.2	(125)
Affiliated Union	0	(0)	34.7	(46)	54.7	(15)

* The data on constituency support for the NDP were taken from the results of the 1979 federal election as reported in Canada, *Report of the Chief Electoral Officer, 1979*.

Data on votes for the NDP, presented in panel B of table 15, reveal a similar pattern – members of NDP-affiliated locals are more inclined to vote for the NDP than are their non-affiliated counterparts, controlling for the constituency strength of the party. Again, in each instance for which there are more than a few cases, the trends are in the anticipated direction. Taken to-

TABLE 16

NDP Leader, Party, and Candidate Thermometer Scores, by Union Status, 1979*

Union Status	Mean Thermometer Score	N
A. Leader (Broadbent)		
Non-Unionist	52.8	(1332)
Member of Non-Affiliated Union	56.8	(879)
Member of Affiliated Union	65.4	(117)
Total Respondents	54.9	(2328)
p <.001 Eta = .13		
B. Local Candidate		
Non-Unionist	41.0	(970)
Member of Non-Affiliated Union	48.4	(698)
Member of Affiliated Union	57.6	(90)
Total Respondents	44.8	(1758)
p <.001 Eta = .19		
C. Party		
Non-Unionist	43.2	(1318)
Member of Non-Affiliated Union	50.6	(881)
Member of Affiliated Union	56.8	(114)
Total Respondents	46.7	(2313)
p <.001 Eta = .17		

* The thermometer score is based on a scale of 1 to 100, with 50 explicitly designated as the neutral position. Scores above 50 indicate positive feelings towards the object in question, while scores below 50 reflect negative evaluations.

gether, these data lend considerable support to the argument that the decision of union locals to affiliate with the NDP has an important independent effect in mobilizing members of that local to support the party.

Recall the hypothesis that affiliation with the NDP affects not only the way individuals vote, but also the way in which they view the social and political world and their place within it. With respect to their feelings towards the New Democratic party, its leader, and its local candidate, the data in table 16 indicate that

TABLE 17
Social Class Awareness and Class Self-Placement,
by Union Status, 1979*

A. Class Awareness (R Thinks of Himself as Member of Class)

	% Yes	% No	N
Non-Unionist	41.3	58.7	(1434)
Member of Non-Affiliated Union	50.9	49.1	(940)
Member of Affiliated Union	45.4	54.6	(123)
Total Respondents	45.1	54.9	(2497)

p <.001

B. Class Self-Placement (%)

	Upper/ Upper Middle	Middle	Working/ Lower	N
Non-Unionist	12.8	53.8	33.4	(1357)
Member of Non-Affiliated Union	9.4	52.6	38.0	(915)
Member of Affiliated Union	7.0	44.0	49.0	(114)
Total Respondents	11.2	52.9	35.0	(2386)

p <.001

* Row percentages

members of NDP-affiliated locals in 1979 felt "warmer" towards the party, its leader (Ed Broadbent), and their local NDP candidate than did their counterparts in non–NDP-affiliated unions.

Because union-party affiliation is a link between working-class organizations and a working-class party, it was hypothesized that union affiliation with the party would increase the extent to which the individuals thought in class terms. Table 17 presents mixed evidence on this question. As panel A indicates, members of NDP-affiliated locals were somewhat less inclined to think of themselves as belonging to a class than were members of non-affiliated locals. However, the data in panel B indicate that when members of NDP-affiliated unions do offer a class view of society, they are more likely to perceive themselves as members of the working or lower class and less likely to ascribe membership in the middle class to themselves. For example, whereas 38 per cent of members of non–NDP-affiliated locals considered themselves working or lower class, 49 per cent of members of NDP-affiliated locals viewed themselves in these terms.

The data in table 18 illustrate that union status also is related to an individual's placement on a left-right self-anchoring scale. Individuals placed themselves on a scale ranging from one (far-

TABLE 18
*Left-Right Subjective Class Self-Placement,
by Union Status, 1979*

Union Status	Mean Left-Right Self-Placement	N
A. Non-Unionist		
Upper/Upper Middle	4.7	(143)
Middle	4.6	(579)
Working/Lower	4.4	(321)
Total Respondents	4.5	(1043)
B. Member of Non-Affiliated Union		
Upper/Upper Middle	4.6	(78)
Middle	4.3	(382)
Working/Lower	4.1	(261)
Total Respondents	4.2	(721)
C. Member of Affiliated Union		
Upper/Upper middle	4.3	(7)
Middle	4.1	(41)
Working/Lower	3.8	(50)
Total Respondents	3.9	(98)

p *.001   Eta = −.12

thest left) to seven (farthest right); therefore the lower the score, the more leftist the orientation of that group. Both non-unionists and members of non–NDP-affiliated union locals had mean scores to the right of centre, whereas for members of NDP-affiliated locals, the mean score was slightly to the left of centre. In addition, the data in table 18 show that within each category, members of the working/lower class were more likely to view themselves as more leftist than their middle, upper-middle, and upper-class counterparts. Thus, the data suggest that membership in an NDP-affiliated local is more often associated with a working-class and leftist self-image.

CONCLUSION

Only a small, and declining, proportion of union members in Canada belong to locals affiliated with the NDP. Contrary to the popular belief that a strong link exists between organized labour and the NDP, the link – as measured by rates of affiliation – is very weak. When the link is present, when unions do affiliate with the NDP, it clearly has a positive effect on levels of NDP support. For example, membership in an NDP-affiliated local was found to be positively related to identification with and vote for the party, and this relationship persisted after controlling for the constituency strength of the party and the type of union to which an individual belonged. Additionally, members of NDP-affiliated locals were found to have more positive evaluations of the NDP, of its leader, and of local NDP candidates. They also were more likely to have a working-class and leftist self-image than their counterparts in unaffiliated locals.

With respect to election outcomes, members of affiliated locals are three to four times more likely to vote NDP than are non-unionists and also significantly more likely to do so than members of non-affiliated unions; nonetheless only a minority of NDP-affiliated unionists voted for the party. Thus, although the electoral importance of union affiliation is both striking and significant, its overall electoral effect is limited. At the aggregate level its importance is limited by the rate of union affiliation with the NDP. Because so few unions or, perhaps more accurately, only unions whose membership constitutes a small proportion of workers have affiliated with the party, only a limited number of voters are even open to this effect. At the individual level, the influence of union affiliation with the party is limited by the very nature of political choice and by the forces which are brought to bear on that choice. To understand this second limitation, it is necessary to explore more fully the dynamics of political choice in Canadian federal elections. The next chapter presents a multivariate analysis, using a dynamic simultaneous equation model of voting which includes a measure of union local affiliation with the NDP.

CHAPTER SIX

Explaining Voting Behaviour in Canada

While the analysis in the previous chapter indicated that membership in an NDP-affiliated union local increased the likelihood of an individual voting NDP, it did not take into account all of the complex factors involved in determining voting choice. In this chapter a model of voting is presented which includes both long-term factors such as membership in an NDP-affiliated union and the short-term forces which come to play during any election campaign.

Recent research on the determinants of voting in American presidential elections has begun to resolve the differences in the approaches to voting behaviour developed by Anthony Downs and by Angus Campbell and his colleagues.[1] This work suggests that a vote represents neither a completely short-term calculation of utility functions and a rational maximization of utilities, nor a product of long-term forces largely immune from short-term factors. Rather, it is a combination of the two, characterized by strong reciprocal effects between long-term and short-term forces.[2] The merger of the models of Downs and Campbell was made possible through the modelling of reciprocal relationships, and the estimation of their parameters via simultaneous equations and two-stage or three-stage least squares regression techniques.

These methodological advances are well suited to studying the determinants of voting in Canada. The short-term variability of long-term factors influencing political choice in Canada, especially the flexibility of partisanship, has been documented time and again. Although for many years the strength of partisan identification was considered the *single* strongest predictor of both the probability and direction of voting in the United States, it has been demonstrated that in Canada partisanship tends to be unstable and subject to change over relatively short periods of time.[3] For example, in their analysis of a three-wave panel study of the Canadian electorate between 1974 and 1980, LeDuc and his colleagues noted:

During the five years between the 1974 and 1979 elections, less than half of the panel (48 percent) was stable with regard to both party identification and vote. Between the 1979 and 1980 elections, the comparable figure is only 58 percent, although these two contests occurred within a nine-month span. This finding suggests that time alone is of limited importance in accounting for partisan instability. Time is seemingly less important than the existence of opportunities for change, such as those provided by exposure to short-term forces generated by events such as elections.[4]

Despite such findings, surprisingly little effort has been directed at structuring a model of voting that attempts to measure the reciprocal effects of partisanship, issue assessment, and candidate evaluation on one another. The model developed here permits these measurements and also facilitates the inclusion of a variety of exogenous variables which may have a direct or indirect effect on voting choice. More specifically, reciprocal relationships among party identification, attitude to issues, and evaluation of the party leaders are estimated, using data from the 1979 national election study. The use of two-stage least squares will also enable the measurement of the electoral importance of union affiliation to the NDP, while taking into account the other major determinants of voting.

A RECIPROCAL MODEL OF CANADIAN VOTING BEHAVIOUR

The model, presented in figure 1, has four endogenous variables: direction of vote, strength and direction of party identification, evaluation of party leaders, and respondents' perceptions of the party closest to them on issues of personal importance. It also includes a large number of exogenous variables, most of which are used to create "instruments" for the endogenous variables.*

---

* *Endogenous variables* are those whose values are determined by the model. In an ordinary least squares equation, they generally are known as dependent variables (that is, they represent the event(s) explained by the model). In a nonrecursive system of equations, endogenous variables may both be dependent

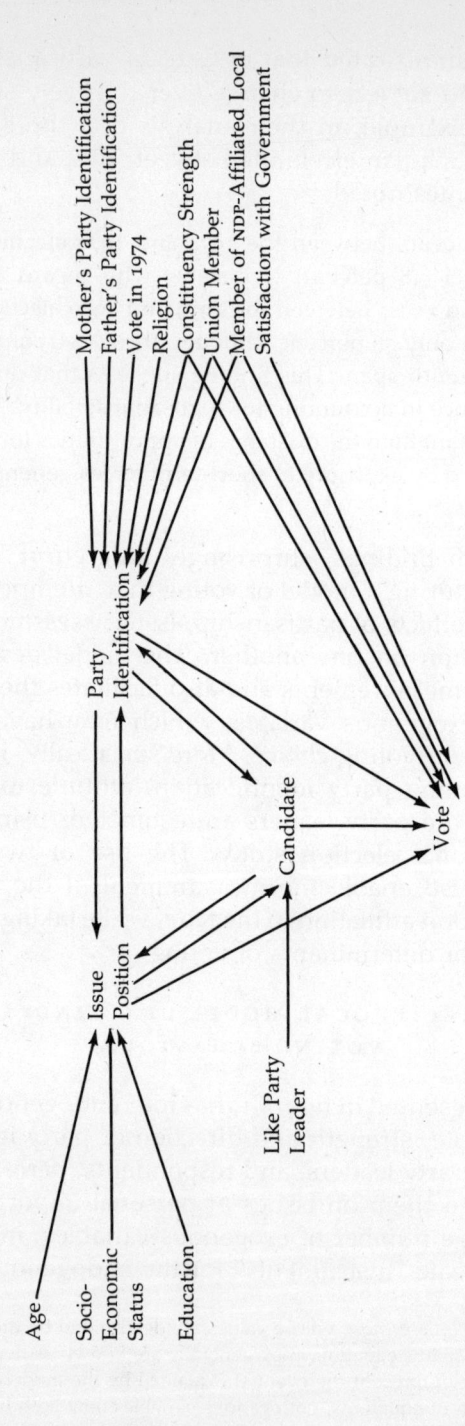

Figure 1. Reciprocal Model of the Determinants of Voting.

This model is based on similar models applied to the United States electorate by Page and Jones and by Markus and Converse. It differs from both of them in that it includes a direct causal path from each of the three attitudinal variables (that is, party, leader, and issues) to vote whereas the former map only the direct effects of candidate evaluation and party identification on vote.[5]

The Page-Jones model was based on a priori theoretical rather than a posteriori statistical criteria and reflects their interpretation of the way in which the American political system operates. They assume that the separation of executive and legislative powers, and the election for the presidency, highlights an evaluation of the candidates as individuals rather than as representatives of parties. Because individuals vote directly for the president, Page and Jones assume that the vote reflects differences in the evaluation of the candidates ($r = .81$), which in turn may be influenced by party identification and position on issues.[6]

In the Canadian parliamentary system of government such an assumption is unwarranted. Canadian voters do not cast their ballots directly for or against the leaders of the several parties. Only the name and party affiliation of the candidates for the House of Commons in their constituency appear on the ballot. The governor general, using prerogative powers, appoints the prime minister. By convention, that individual is the person most able to command majority support in the house and is usually, although not always, the leader of the party with a plurality of seats in the house. Although individual voters may base voting decisions on their evaluation of party leaders, their votes may also be "party" votes. Consequently, this model leaves open the possibility of a direct causal link between identification and vote for a political party.

Unlike the Page-Jones and Markus-Converse models, this model posits a direct causal link between respondents' perceptions of the party closest to them on the issue(s) most important to them and vote. There is no strong theoretical justification for

---

variables (that is, they may be predicted by the model) and be used in turn to predict the values of other variables. See, for example, Hanushek and Jackson, *Statistical Methods for Social Scientists*, 225–8. For a further discussion and application, see Erlanger and Winsborough, "The Structure of Violence Thesis"; and Wanner and Lewis, "The Functional Theory of Stratification." *Exogenous variables* usually are referred to as independent variables. Their values are determined outside of the model and are taken as given. See Hanushek and Jackson, *Statistical Methods for Social Scientists*, 225–8.

expecting the effects of the evaluation of party positions on issues to be mediated through evaluations of the party leaders. Indeed, previous analyses of the 1979 Canadian federal election have demonstrated that many voters gave very positive evaluations to the issue position of the Conservative party while giving much lower grades to its leader, Joe Clark.[7] In addition, a substantial proportion of voters were labelled "durable" partisans, individuals whose party identification is less susceptible to change because of short-term issue positions.[8] In short, although perceptions of the parties' positions on issues may be mediated through evaluations of the party leaders and through party identification, they also may have a direct effect on voting.

Accordingly, the model hypothesizes a two-way causal path between each of the endogenous attitudinal determinants of voting, and a direct causal path from each of them to the vote.

Figure 1 also shows the exogenous variables used to create instruments of the endogenous determinants of voting. Seven exogenous variables are used to predict party identification. The conceptualization of party identification by Campbell and his colleagues placed a great emphasis on its stability and its intergenerational transmission through family-centred socialization. Although the passing of party identification from one generation to the next has been found to be much weaker in Canada than in the United States,[9] the inclusion of parents' party identification in the model enabled us to gauge its relative importance in directly determining a respondent's partisanship and indirectly determining the other endogenous variables.

In an attempt to measure the stability of party identification, a measure of vote in the 1974 federal election was included. Because partisan identifications are quite "durable" for some 35 per cent of the electorate, we expected this durability to be represented in part by relatively strong coefficients between present identification and past vote.

Many studies have documented the conventional wisdom that religion is an important determinant of voting in Canada.[10] Catholics tend disproportionately to support the Liberal party and Protestants, the Conservative and New Democratic parties. To the extent that religion has an impact on direction of vote, it should be manifest as a long-term force, and hence it was included as a predictor of party identification.

Many studies have illustrated the importance of a contextual variable in determining individual voting choice. For example,

Schwartz, and Engelmann and Schwartz, demonstrate that province or region of residence remains an important determinant of partisan choice in Canada. A related variable which Clarke and his co-workers found to be a relatively important predictor of the vote is the size of the community in which an individual resides: support for the Progressive Conservative and Social Credit/Créditiste parties is greatest in rural communities whereas the NDP receives a disproportionate share of its support from urban communities. Zipp, for his part, defined the contextual variable as the level of support received by the parties in the constituency in which the individual resides.[11] These variables – region/province of residence, size of community, and constituency support for the party – are different ways of measuring the same underlying concept, namely, the extent to which an individual's vote is determined by the social and political environment of which he or she is a part.[12] For example, in areas (that is, regions, provinces, communities, constituencies) in which a party performs very poorly at the polls, its local candidate may not present as viable an alternative to the incumbent as would be the case in areas in which the party is very competitive.[13] Because the measure used by Zipp is a more accurate representation of this underlying contextual dimension, it is used in the present analysis as a determinant of party identification.

The two remaining exogenous variables used to predict party identification are whether an individual (or family member) is a union member and whether he is a member of a union local affiliated with the NDP. Although most studies of voting behaviour in Canada have tended not to include union membership, or NDP-affiliated local membership, the analysis in chapter 5 indicated that they are related to vote and to party identification. These seven exogenous variables represent the long-term component of party identification.

The two endogenous variables – perception of the party closest on important issues, and evaluation of party leaders – are the short-term determinants of party identification. The issue position variable is predicted by three exogenous variables (age, socioeconomic status, and education) and two endogenous variables (party identification and evaluation of party leaders). Although little work has been done on mapping the socio-demographic determinants of issue position in Canada (research has tended to focus on attitudinal determinants such as party identification and evaluation of leaders), Kornberg and Archer have shown that socio-economic status, age, and level of education were related to attitudes towards various constitutional options among the Quebec electorate.[14] Specifically, those with higher levels of education, middle-aged and older respondents, and those with a higher socio-economic status were more likely to have a position on various constitutional options than were those with the opposite attributes. It is thus expected that individuals with these attributes will be more likely than their counterparts to name issues which they think are personally important and to identify the party they feel is closest to them on these issues.

Evaluation of party leaders is predicted by one exogenous variable – whether the individual likes the personal characteristics of a party's leader – and two endogenous variables: party identification and perceptions of the party closest on important issues. It was more difficult to select variables which could serve as instruments for the leaders evaluation variable because of the tendency for predictors of feelings towards a party leader to be correlated with party identification, and hence the estimated coefficients were biased and unreliable. Although the explained variance (R^2) in each instance was stronger when feelings towards the party were used instead of the variable measuring the respondent's feelings towards the leader's personal characteristics, the accompanying bias in the estimates negated the benefits of a better fitting model.

Direction of the vote is predicted by three endogenous variables (party identification, evaluation of the party leaders, and perception of the party closest on issues of personal importance) and four exogenous variables (constituency strength of the party, union membership, membership in an NDP-affiliated union local, and satisfaction with the incumbent government's performance). I have commented above on the reasons for using the three endogenous variables. Regarding the exogenous variables, constituency strength of the party is used because it is expected that individuals will be more likely to vote for a party in those constituencies in which the party is competitive. Union membership and membership in an NDP-affiliated union local are used because previous analysis indicated that they were related to the direction of voting. The satisfaction with government variable is included to test a version of the "retrospective voting" thesis. In his analysis of the structure underlying voting decisions in the United States, Fiorina argued that retrospective judgments of the performance of incumbent administrations have a greater impact than expectations based on the policy platforms of the competing parties.[15] The hypothesis is that those who are more satisfied with the incumbent government's performance are more likely to vote for that party than are those who are less satisfied.

Finally, consistency of identification with a political party – that is, identification with the same party at the federal and provincial levels – was included in the analysis as was a class variable (whether an individual thought of himself as a member of the working/lower class). However, neither variable was found to be a significant predictor either of vote or of the attitudinal determinants of voting, and thus they were excluded from the analysis. (Consistency was not used to predict party identification because of their partial identity.) The absence of a relationship between consistency of party identification and voting underscores the distinction which most Canadians maintain between federal and provincial political parties.[16]

MEASURES AND METHODS

Using this model of Canadian voting behaviour, the coefficients for each path were estimated for the Liberal, Progressive Conservative, and New Democratic parties (presented in tables 19, 20, and 21, respectively). In each case, the vote variable is dichotomous (for example, NDP voters versus all others). The party identification variable ranges from 0 to 3, with zero representing, for example, non-NDP identifiers; one, weak NDP identifiers; two, moderate NDP identifiers; and three, strong NDP identifiers. The leader variable is a simple thermometer rating (0 to 100) of the leader of the party under study. It was thought that this usage was preferable to a weighted combination of all leaders' thermometer scores because in a three-party system the latter might lead to incorrect inferences.* Father's and mother's party identifications are dichotomous variables. The religion variable is di-

---

* To take an extreme example, suppose Trudeau was rated 100, Clark rated 0, and Broadbent rated 50. A weighted score for Broadbent, calculated as (Leader C - (leader A + leader B + leader C) / 3) = Broadbent rating, would yield the same result as would the score from evaluations of Trudeau = 50, Clark = 50, and Broadbent = 50, despite the very different ratings of the candidates. Although using the single-candidate thermometer rating is not statistically better than the weighted score, it may be inferentially superior.

chotomous (that is, Catholic (1) and non-Catholic (0)). The "feelings about party" variable was constructed in an analogous manner. Satisfaction with the government is an index which measures an individual's material and general well-being, and the government's impact thereon.* The issue position variable ranges from 0 to 2. Respondents were asked which issues were most and second most important to them personally in the election, and which party was closest to them on each of those issues. For the NDP example, those who stated that the NDP was closest to them on both issues were coded two, those who said it was closest on one issue were coded one, and those who didn't mention the NDP were coded zero. The variable was measured in a similar way for the Liberal and Conservative parties. Socio-economic status is a four-digit summary estimated by Blishen and McRoberts.[17] Age is measured in years, and education in years of formal education. Both union membership and membership in NDP-affiliated locals are dichotomous variables. Constituency strength for each party was derived from the report of the chief electoral officer, and percentages were rounded to one decimal point. Finally, all variables were standardized (that is, mean = 0; standard deviation = 1). The coefficients in tables 19-21 are two-stage least squares regression coefficients and are presented in both standardized and unstandardized form.

Before proceeding with the data analysis, it may be useful to provide a brief summary of the context within which the 1979 national election study was conducted. In the election of 22 May 1979, the Progressive Conservative party under Joe Clark's leadership won 136 of 282 seats in the House of Commons on the basis of 36 per cent of the popular vote. The Liberal party received 40 per cent of the popular vote, but won only 114 seats in the house. The NDP won 26 seats and 18 per cent of the popular vote, and the Social Credit/Créditiste party received 5 per cent of the vote and 6 seats. The Conservatives (although six seats

* Respondents were asked whether: (1) they were satisfied or dissatisfied with their current economic condition and lives more generally, and (2) government had any effect on their condition. Responses were scored as follows: very satisfied = 2; fairly satisfied = 1; a little dissatisfied = −1; very dissatisfied = −2. These scores were multiplied by government's perceived impact responses which were scored as follows: a great deal = 2; some = 1; not much = 0. The resulting index ranges from +4 to −4. A comparable index was generated for general life satisfaction, and the two measures were combined to yield an overall index with scores ranging from +8 to −8. For a previous application of this scale, see Kornberg et al, "Federalism and Fragmentation."

short of a majority) formed the government for the first time since the 1963 election.

The 1979 national election was the first fought by the Conservatives under the leadership of Joe Clark and by the NDP under Ed Broadbent. The Liberal party had gone into the election under the leadership of Pierre Trudeau who had been leader of the party and prime minister since 1968. In the previous election, held on 8 July 1974, the Liberals had been returned with a majority after two years as a minority government. The Liberal government had delayed calling an election until its mandate was about to expire. The reluctance to call an election was widely attributed at the time to a poor showing in public opinion polls.

Previous analyses of the 1979 election results have attributed the Conservative victory to that party's ability to capitalize on a number of short-term issues, including the "issue" of Trudeau's leadership.[18] That analysis would appear to be substantiated by the defeat of the Conservative government in the ensuing election which occurred only nine months after it assumed office.

DATA ANALYSIS

Table 19 presents data on the determinants of voting for the Liberal party in 1979.* They indicate that identification with the Liberal party explained almost all of the variance in Liberal vote. Those who identified with the Liberal party, and identified strongly, were much more likely to vote for the Liberals than were weak or non-Liberal identifiers. In addition, those who evaluated Trudeau very positively were more likely than not to vote Liberal, although this attitude is less important than party identification. Interestingly, there is a negative relationship between identifying the Liberals as the party closest on personally important issues and voting Liberal, suggesting that many people voted Liberal in 1979 despite perceiving another party or no party as closest on the important issues of the campaign.

---

* To maximize the number of cases analysed in the model, the mean substitution procedure has been used for missing data, the effect of which has been to "flatten" the regression line. Although this procedure weakened the model overall, the eightfold increase in the number of cases used in the analysis greatly increased confidence in the reliability of the results. Interestingly, in all but a few instances, the relative strength of the coefficients has been unaffected. Note that the explained variance (R^2) presented at the bottom of each table corresponds to the "vote" equation.

TABLE 19
Reciprocal Model of Liberal Vote, 1979
(two-stage least squares estimates)

Dependent Variable Prediction Variables	Unstandardized Parameter Estimate	Standard Error	Standardized Parameter Estimate
A. Vote			
Intercept	−.106	.07	
Leader	.004	.00	.14**
Issues	−.158	.09	−.09*
Party Identification	.370	.03	.54***
Constituency Strength	.001	.000	.04**
Satisfaction with Government	.004	.003	.02
Union Member	−.002	.01	.00
Member of NDP-Affiliated Local	−.002	.04	.00
B. Leader			
Intercept	34.750	0.83	
Issues	17.411	6.09	.15***
Party Identification	16.410	2.04	.37***
Like Trudeau	2.710	0.64	.09***
C. Issues			
Intercept	−.607	.11	
Leader	.009	.00	.23***
Party Identification	.140	.06	.15**
Socio-Economic Status	.004	.00	.71**
Age	.001	.00	.01
Education	.013	.00	.06***
D. Party Identification			
Intercept	−1.053	.19	
Leader	.020	.01	.29***
Issues	−.329	.33	−.07
Father's Party Identification	.193	.06	.06***
Mother's Party Identification	.205	.07	.06***
Vote in 1974	.903	.10	.33***
Religion	−.100	.05	−.04*
Constituency Strength	.005	.00	.08***
Union Member	.004	.04	.00
Member of NDP Affiliated Local	.084	.09	.01

$R^2 = .37$; N = 2,761
* p*.10; ** p*.05; *** p*.01

The other significant predictor of voting for the Liberal party was the strength of the Liberals in the constituency in which the individual resided. The stronger the party's performance in a given constituency (such as a Quebec constituency), the more likely that individual was to vote for the party. Although the constituency strength of the party was a weaker predictor than attitudinal characteristics, nonetheless its effect was statistically significant, and its standard error was small.

Evaluation of Pierre Trudeau as a party leader was influenced strongly by Liberal party identification, feelings about his personal qualities, and the party's issue position. The effect of party identification on evaluation of Trudeau was very strong and accounted for more of the variance than the other predictors. Those who liked Trudeau's personal qualities were also much more likely to evaluate him positively than those who did not. Finally, those who perceived that the positions of the Liberal party on issues important to them were closest to their own were likely to have a more positive evaluation of Trudeau than those who perceived another party as closest. However, it should be noted that there is a larger error for this than for the other predictors of feelings towards Trudeau. This suggests that although many individuals who felt the Liberal positions most closely corresponded with their own evaluated Trudeau positively, many others evaluated Trudeau positively despite perceiving that another party's positions on issues were closest to their own.

The strongest predictor of whether voters felt the Liberal party was closest to their own position on issues was their evaluation of Trudeau. Identification with the Liberal party also had a significant effect on perceptions of the Liberals as the party closest on important issues. The data also indicate that socio-economic status and education were significant predictors of the issues variable. As expected, those individuals with higher levels of education and higher socio-economic status were more likely to have positions on issues and to perceive that the positions of the Liberal party on those issues were closest to their own than were individuals with the opposite attributes.

Panel D of table 19 presents data on the determinants of Liberal party identification in 1979. It is notable that short-term attitudinal determinants were strong predictors of Liberal party identification. In particular, the evaluation of Trudeau was very strongly related to party identification; those who felt warmly towards Trudeau were the most likely to identify, and identify strongly, with the Liberals. The data also suggest that many individuals who did not perceive the Liberals as closest to their own positions on important issues nonetheless identified with the Liberal party. That is, the issues variable is a *negative* and non-significant predictor of Liberal identification. On the surface, this finding is counter-intuitive, suggesting that the Liberal party could increase its number of party identifiers by adopting positions on issues which were not congruent with those of the electorate. A more plausible explanation is that for some voters party identification operates in a manner consistent with the formulation of Campbell and his colleagues – that is, it is resistant to fluctuations in short-term variables.

The latter interpretation is buttressed by the finding that several long-term variables are significantly related to identification with the Liberal party. In particular, a vote for the Liberal party in 1974 (interpreted as a long-term variable) was strongly related to Liberal identification in 1979. When the analysis was repeated using only the panel component of the survey (that is, excluding newly eligible voters), the strength of 1974 vote increased by approximately one-third (data not shown). In addition, the constituency strength of the Liberal party and parents' party identifications were weak to moderately significant predictors of identification with the party.

Table 20 presents data on the determinants of Progressive Conservative party vote in the 1979 federal election. As in the Liberal case, identification with the Conservative party was the strongest predictor of voting for that party, although the importance of party identification was somewhat less than for the Liberals. However, in marked contrast to the Liberal vote, the perception that the party was closest on personally important issues was a relatively strong positive predictor of Conservative voting. Again in contrast to the Liberals, feelings towards the party leader, Joe Clark, were not related to Conservative voting. The data also suggest that constituency strength of the Conservative party *and* membership in an NDP-affiliated union local were significant predictors of Conservative vote. With respect to the latter, the relationship was negative, suggesting that affiliated union members were less likely to vote for the party than were other

TABLE 20
Reciprocal Model
of Progressive Conservative Vote, 1979
(two-stage least squares estimates)

Dependent Variable Prediction Variables	Unstandardized Parameter Estimate	Standard Error	Standardized Parameter Estimate
A. Vote			
Intercept	.045	.06	
Leader	.009	.00	.02
Issues	.250	.05	.17***
Party Identification	.300	.03	.42***
Constituency Strength	.009	.00	.04**
Satisfaction with Government	−.001	.00	−.01
Union Member	−.016	.01	−.02
Member of NDP-Affiliated Local	−.065	.03	−.03*
B. Leader			
Intercept	41.737	.66	
Issues	−5.882	3.31	−.08*
Party Identification	15.691	1.44	.43***
Like Clark	5.404	.61	.18***
C. Issues			
Intercept	−1.170	.13	
Leader	.019	.00	.32***
Party Identification	.123	.04	.12***
Socio-Economic Status	.004	.00	.07***
Age	−.002	.00	.00
Education	.025	.00	.14***
D. Party Identification			
Intercept	−.704	.12	
Leader	.013	.00	.15***
Issues	.072	.13	.02
Father's Party Identification	.221	.05	.08***
Mother's Party Identification	.171	.06	.06***
Vote in 1974	1.102	.07	.42***
Religion	−.025	.04	−.01
Constituency Strength	.004	.00	.08***
Union Member	−.055	.03	−.03*
Member of NDP Affiliated Local	−.006	.07	.00

R^2 = .38; N = 2,761
* p<.10; ** p<.05; *** p<.01

voters. Thus, a Conservative party vote in 1979 appears to have been the product of a combination of short- and long-term forces, with the impact of issue position and party identification contributing the most to the party's victory.

The data in panel B of table 20 indicate that, as in the Liberal party, evaluations of Clark were most strongly determined by Conservative identification and response to Clark's personal qualities. Conservative identifiers, especially those with strong identifications, were more likely to evaluate Clark positively than were non- and weak Conservative identifiers. Also, as one would expect, those who liked Clark's personal qualities were more likely to feel "warmer" towards him than those who did not.

Although issue position was not significantly related to evaluation of Clark, the latter was strongly related to perceptions of the Conservative party as closest on important issues. Those who evaluated Clark positively invariably also felt the Conservatives were closest on important issues. The data also indicate that Conservative identifiers, those with higher socio-economic status, and those with higher levels of education were more likely to view the Conservative party as closest on issues. However, in comparison with the Liberals, the effect of party identification relative to other predictors of issue position is relatively weak among those feeling the Conservative party was closest on issues.

The determinants of Conservative identification are presented in panel D of table 20. Whereas evaluation of Trudeau was a very strong and significant predictor of Liberal party identification, evaluation of Clark was a much weaker and less significant predictor of Conservative identification. For the Liberals, there was a strong two-way relationship between identification with the party and a positive evaluation of Trudeau, whereas for the Conservatives, the relationship was much stronger from identification with the party to evaluation of the party leader than vice versa. Also in contrast to the negative relationship between issue position and Liberal identification, there was a moderately positive relationship between perceptions of the Conservatives as closest on issues and identification with the party. The most important determinant of Conservative identification was long-term partisanship, measured by 1974 vote. Among the other long-term determinants, parents' party identification and constituency strength also were significant predictors of current identification.

TABLE 21
Reciprocal Model
of New Democratic Vote 1979
(two-stage least squares estimates)

Dependent Variable Prediction Variables	Unstandardized Parameter Estimate	Standard Error	Standardized Parameter Estimate
A. Vote			
Intercept	.014	.05	
Leader	.000	.00	.00
Issues	.121	.22	.06
Party Identification	.360	.07	.49***
Constituency Strength	.002	.000	.07***
Satisfaction with Government	−.002	.002	−.01
Union Member	.007	.01	.01
Member of NDP-Affiliated Local	−.020	.03	−.01
B. Leader			
Intercept	46.860	.72	
Issues	44.048	12.11	.32***
Party Identification	−2.537	4.35	−.05
Like Broadbent	5.095	.52	.19***
C. Issues			
Intercept	−.102	.06	
Leader	.001	.00	.02
Party Identification	.345	.03	.36***
Socio-Economic Status	.003	.00	.01
Age	.003	.00	.01
Education	.007	.00	.06**
D. Party Identification			
Intercept	−.205	.15	
Leader	.002	.00	.03
Issues	.383	.52	.09
Father's Party Identification	.174	.12	.05
Mother's Party Identification	.227	.10	.05**
Vote in 1974	1.270	.23	.47***
Religion	.038	.02	.03
Constituency Strength	.005	.00	.08***
Union Member	.053	.03	.04*
Member of NDP Affiliated Local	.172	.06	.05***

$R^2 = .33$; N = 2,761
* p<.10; ** p<.05; *** p<.01

Table 21 presents data on the determinants of the vote for the NDP in the 1979 election. Panel A indicates that identification with the NDP was strongly related to NDP vote. Evaluation of Ed Broadbent and perceptions of the NDP as the party closest on important issues were not significantly related to voting for the NDP, controlling for the effects of party identification. The data also indicate that constituency strength was a significant predictor of NDP voting, whereas satisfaction with the government and the two union variables were not.

The data in panel B indicate that, in contrast to both the Liberals and Conservatives, increasing strength of NDP identification did not produce increasingly positive evaluations of Broadbent. Perception of the NDP as the party closest on important issues, however, was strongly related to positive evaluation of Broadbent. In addition, those who liked Broadbent's personal qualities were more likely to feel "warmer" towards him.

The data in panel C indicate that NDP identifiers were more likely to perceive the NDP as closest on important issues. The relationship between evaluation of Broadbent and perception of the NDP as closest on important issues was not significant and considerably weaker than the analogous relationships for the Liberal and Conservative parties. The relationship between party identification and perceptions of closeness on issues was stronger for the NDP than for either the Liberals or Conservatives.

Panel D presents data on the determinants of NDP identification in 1979. Closeness on important issues was not significantly related to identification with the NDP, suggesting that many individuals either identified with the NDP despite feeling another party best represented their position on issues or identified with another party despite feeling that the NDP was closest. The ability of party identification to predict feelings of closeness on issues suggests the latter interpretation is probably correct. Nor was evaluation of the party leader a strong or significant predictor of identification with the NDP. Indeed, long-term factors were much more important than short-term ones in predicting NDP identification. A vote for the party in 1974 was by far the strongest predictor of NDP identification in 1979, suggesting that party identification may be more stable for NDP identifiers than for those identifying with the Liberal or Conservative party. The constituency strength of the NDP, mother's party identification, and membership in a union local affiliated with the party were also significantly related to NDP identification.

Although membership in an NDP-affiliated local is a significant predictor of identification with the NDP, its relationship to both NDP identification and vote was weaker than anticipated. Three factors, two substantive and the other statistical, may help account for the relative weakness of this variable. First, although members of affiliated locals were more likely to support the NDP than members of non-affiliated locals, many of the former supported the Liberal party. Second, the strongest single trend throughout this analysis has been the strength of attitudinal and the weakness of socio-demograhic variables in explaining political behaviour. In comparison with other socio-demographic variables, however, the strength of membership in an affiliated local is quite impressive. Third, the number of individuals who are members of union locals affiliated with the NDP is very small in the Canadian electorate (3 per cent) and in the sample under study (5 per cent). Because this group makes up a very small proportion of the sample, it simply cannot explain a large proportion of the variance.

In sum, the data indicate that attitudes were the most significant predictors of NDP vote, and identification with the party was the strongest of these. Identification with the party was more a product of long-term forces in the case of the NDP than it was for the Liberal and Conservative parties. Issue position in the 1979 campaign worked against both the NDP and the Liberals and favoured the Conservatives.

As noted in chapter 5, the way in which the union variable was measured in the 1984 national election study prevents the replication of this model of voting using the 1984 data. With fewer than 70 cases of affiliated union members in the data set, the coefficients for union affiliation are likely to be unstable. However, a similar analysis was conducted by the principal investigators of the 1984 national election study, with the important caveat that their union membership variable made no attempt to differentiate members of affiliated locals. Their results are consistent with mine. They found that union membership was a significant and positive predictor of NDP identification and their coefficient was of almost exactly the same magnitude as the coefficient in my analysis. Similarly, they found that union membership was not directly related to voting for the NDP. Rather, its effect is indirect, acting through party identification, which was by far the single strongest predictor of NDP voting.[19] The data from 1979 suggest that that effect would be strengthened if it were possible to isolate membership in an NDP-affiliated union.

CONCLUSION

This analysis has illuminated the strength of the various determinants of voting in a Canadian election. Perhaps most significant was the finding of substantial diversity among the three parties in the relative effects of variables. For example, although party identification was the strongest determinant of voting for each party in 1979, issue position played a crucial role for the Conservatives, who benefited from the fact that large numbers of Canadians thought that party was closest to them on important issues, whereas evaluation of the party leader was beneficial to the Liberal party. With respect to issues, it also is noteworthy that the Liberals and New Democrats were able to withstand relatively negative evaluations on issue position from their partisans. For both parties in 1979, issue position was negatively or not significantly related to party identification, indicating that many individuals chose to support "their" party despite their response to short-term factors.

Second, it was found that the attitudinal determinants of voting tended to be strongly related to one another. It is noteworthy that party identification is more strongly influenced by evaluation of party leader than by the perceived issue position of the party. Consequently, the outcomes of both the 1979 and 1980 national elections are not especially surprising. The Conservative party was able to capitalize on its strong standing on issues in 1979 but was unable to transform that advantage into either more positive evaluation of the party leader or a higher rate of identification. Nine months later, without a favourable issue position, the Conservative government was defeated by the Trudeau-led Liberals.

Finally, it should be noted that attitudes were much more important determinants of voting, and of one another, than were socio-demographic characteristics. This is consistent with previous analyses which have highlighted the importance of psychological and the weakness of socio-demographic variables in determining Canadian voting behaviour. However, more recently there has been a resurgence in analyses which are designed to explore more fully the effect of socio-demographic variables once they have been more fully mobilized.[20]

The treatment of the union affiliation variable is in keeping with these analyses. The rules on union affiliation with the NDP have a strong historical grounding and were worked out in the 1930s and early 1940s in the CCF. When the NDP was created, it incorporated these established rules of affiliation but also adopted a renewed commitment to strengthening the affiliation movement. However, of all the links that exist between labour and the party, affiliation remains the weakest. The reason for this weakness may have much less to do with the political commitment of unionists and more to do with the pay-off of affiliation for each union local. In the end, each union local must decide. It has also been shown that the decision on affiliation has consequences in Canadian electoral politics. The Canadian electorate displays a great deal of partisan fluidity, and, for many, political allegiance is open to significant variation. One of the forces that can help stabilize partisan allegiance is for significant groups to channel consistent political information, messages, and cues to their members. These cues do not solidify the political preferences of all group members, but their effect is both substantively and statistically significant. On a shifting and sometimes perilous political sea, they provide both a chart and a safe harbour for voters. They should not be ignored by political analysts.

Notes

CHAPTER ONE

1 Hartz, *The Founding of New Societies*; and Horowitz, *Canadian Labour in Politics*. For a historical perspective on this tradition see Forbes, "Hartz-Horowitz at Twenty." A much more fully developed discussion of the various approaches to understanding class politics in Canada can be found in Pammett, "Class Voting and Class Consciousness in Canada."
2 Bell, "The Loyalist Tradition in Canada."
3 Horowitz, *Canadian Labour in Politics*, 262.
4 This perspective informs the work of Brodie and Jenson, *Crisis, Challenge and Change*. This position also can be found in Cairns, "The Governments and Societies of Canadian Federalism."
5 As the National Committee for the New Party stated: "a central organization like the Canadian Labour Congress, which itself is made up almost entirely of affiliated organizations, will not be affiliated to the new party as a Congress. Individual trade unions will each make their own democratic decision whether to affiliate to the party or not. If they decide in favour, they will be affiliated to the CLC for economic purposes and to the party for political purposes. It is important to keep the two functions separate. The Congress and the new party will undoubtedly have a very friendly relationship with each other, but in all probability there will be no formal ties between them. This is the situation in Great Britain and other democratic countries." (Quoted in Horowitz, *Canadian Labour in*

Politics, 242.) For a reiteration of this position, once the NDP had been established, see the lead editorial in *Canadian Labour* 6 (September 1961), the official journal of the CLC, on the occasion of the NDP's founding convention.

6 The Trades and Labor Congress (TLC) merged with the Canadian Congress of Labour (CCL) in 1956 to form the Canadian Labour Congress (CLC) which, as of 1982, represented 57.6 per cent of organized labour in Canada (Labour Canada, *Directory of Labour Organizations*, 1982, 19). It should be noted that the description of the CLC as a united working-class movement necessarily is a relative one. Over 40 per cent of union members in Canada in 1982 belonged to unions not affiliated with the CLC. A disproportionate share of the latter resided in the province of Quebec, in which many of the union federations are affiliated with French-speaking union centrals. Thus, a more accurate description might be a united English-speaking working-class movement.

7 Hartz, *The Founding of New Societies*; McRae, "The Structure of Canadian History"; and Horowitz, *Canadian Labour in Politics*.

8 Barry, *Sociologists, Economists and Democracy*, especially chaps. 1 and 2. See also Olson, *The Logic of Collective Action*.

9 LeDuc, "Canada: The Politics of Stable Dealignment," and LeDuc et al, "Partisan Instability in Canada." As LeDuc notes ("Partisan Change and Dealignment in Canada, Great Britain and the United States," 379): "Dealignment describes a process of weakening or erosion of an existing party alignment without necessarily implying its replacement by a new and stable set of partisan loyalties."

CHAPTER TWO

1 McDonald, *The Party That Changed Canada*.
2 Gibbins, *Conflict and Unity*, 98.
3 Reid, "National Parties," 16–17.
4 Lewis and Scott, *Make This Your Canada*, 115–16.
5 Knowles, *The New Party*, 24–5.
6 Lewis and Scott, *Make This Your Canada*, 118.
7 McNaught, *A Prophet in Politics*, 261.
8 Young, *Anatomy of a Party*, 141.

9 Brodie and Jenson, *Crisis, Challenge and Change*, 130–6.
10 Horowitz, *Canadian Labour in Politics*, 64.
11 Statistics Canada, *Census*, 1931 (author's tabulations).
12 Labour Canada, *Directory of Labour Organizations*, 1973.
13 Horowitz, *Canadian Labour in Politics*, 64; McNaught, *A Prophet in Politics*, 261–2.
14 Lewis, *The Good Fight*, 161.
15 Ibid., 147–8.
16 Horowitz, *Canadian Labour in Politics*, 68.
17 Walter Young described the role of David Lewis thusly: "Lewis, by dint of prodigious energy, remarkable intelligence, and extraordinary persuasive oratory, was able to shape party structure and policy with remarkable freedom ... Lewis dominated the socialist elite, as he did the whole party ... It was largely through his efforts that organized labour came to support the CCF as it did." *Anatomy of a Party*, 163–5.
18 Lewis, *The Good Fight*, 490
19 Ibid., 147–8.
20 Ibid., 71. See also Morton, *NDP: The Dream of Power*, 17.
21 Horowitz, *Canadian Labour in Politics*, 71–2.
22 Lewis, *The Good Fight*, 141–2. Lewis was convinced that the rules of affiliation, and the manner in which organized labour was linked to the party more generally, were sufficient impediments to labour domination. He notes: "Personally, I sometimes wished that labour would show a desire to dominate. I never had any doubt that we could defeat such an attempt, but it would have been evidence of a more earnest commitment to effective political action." *The Good Fight*, 492.
23 Ibid., 192–5.
24 Provincial election results cited in this book are from Simerl, "A Survey of Canadian Provincial Election Results."
25 Morley, *Secular Socialists*, 54–5.
26 Horowitz, *Canadian Labour in Politics*, 80–1. See also Wiseman, *Social Democracy in Manitoba*, 79–80.
27 Young, *Anatomy of a Party*, 83.
28 Morton, *NDP: The Dream of Power*, 18.
29 Horowitz, *Canadian Labour in Politics*, 82.
30 Lewis, *The Good Fight*, 261.

31 Clarke et al., *Political Choice in Canada*, 307-8, and "Voting Behaviour and the Outcome of the 1979 Federal Election," 520-2, for a discussion of transient voters.
32 Horowitz, *Canadian Labour in Politics*, 82-3.
33 For federal election results cited in this book, see Thorburn, ed, *Party Politics in Canada*, 338-49.
34 Horowitz, *Canadian Labour in Politics*, 181.
35 Lewis, *The Good Fight*, 438.
36 Ibid., 440.
37 Ibid., 495.
38 Both documents are reprinted in the appendix of Zakuta, *A Protest Movement Becalmed*, 160-73.
39 Horowitz, *Canadian Labour in Politics*, 198.
40 For a further discussion of the debate on the status of constituency versus affiliated party members, see Morley, *Secular Socialists*, 109-12.
41 NDP, constitution, article VI.3.1 and VI.4.
42 Wiseman, *Social Democracy in Manitoba*, 152.
43 Lewis, *The Good Fight*, 504; see also Morley, *Secular Socialists*, 111-12.
44 Horowitz, *Canadian Labour in Politics*, 221.
45 Wiseman, *Social Democracy in Manitoba*, 115.
46 Morton, *NDP: The Dream of Power*, 32.

CHAPTER THREE

1 Morley, *Secular Socialists*, 109-12.
2 Article VI.5 of the NDP's constitution states that "central labour bodies composed of affiliated organizations, and not eligible for direct affiliation to the Party ... shall be entitled to representation as follows: one delegate from each such central labour body and two delegates from each such central national and provincial body."
3 Archer and Whitehorn, "Opinion Structure among NDP Activists," table 1.
4 NDP files, "Report of the Credentials Committee," selected years.
5 Wiseman, *Social Democracy in Manitoba*, 102-4.
6 Ibid., 117.
7 Interview with Bill Knight, federal secretary of the NDP, 19 September 1988.

8 Lewis, *The Good Fight*, 298–303.
9 Morton, *NDP: The Dream of Power*, 22–3.
10 Morton, *The New Democrats 1961–1986*, 53–6; Morley, *Secular Socialists*, 83–100.
11 For a more detailed discussion, see Stanbury, "The Mother's Milk of Politics," 797–8.
12 Wearing, *Strained Relations*, 181–2.
13 Interview with Knight, 19 September 1988.
14 Data are presented for the period 1979–86 to illustrate the important differences in party fund-raising in election years and non-election years. For the period 1974 to 1978 see Stanbury, "The Mother's Milk of Politics."
15 Data are from Elections Canada, *Federal Parties Fiscal Period Returns, 1974–1986*.
16 Wiseman, *Social Democracy in Manitoba*, 80.
17 Horowitz, *Canadian Labour in Politics*, 80; Labour Canada, *Labour Organizations in Canada, 1977*, xviii.
18 Morley, *Secular Socialists*, 111–12.
19 NDP files, minutes of Federal Executive Meeting, 22–23 August 1962.
20 NDP files, report of NDP-CLC meeting, 3 December 1964.
21 NDP files, letter by George Home, director of political education, CLC, 22 January 1971.
22 NDP files, recommendations endorsed by the Canadian Labour Congress Executive Council Meetings of 3–5 December 1968 and 17–20 February 1969.
23 NDP files, letters from Clifford Scotton to Olive Smith, co-ordinator, political action committee of the Textile Workers Union of America, 16 February 1967; to Neil Reimer, director, District 9, Oil, Chemical and Atomic Workers, 27 February 1970; and to L. Henry Lorrain, 1st vice-president, International Brotherhood of Pulp, Sulphite and Paper Mill Workers, 2 March 1970.
24 NDP files, letters from Michael Lewis (25 March 1966) and C.C. (Doc) Ames (30 March 1966) to Terry Grier.
25 Labour Canada, *Labour Organizations in Canada, 1977*, xix.
26 For example, at NDP conventions held between 1973 and 1981, less than one-quarter (24.2 per cent) of those with credentials from affiliated unions actually attended the convention: NDP files, "Report of the Credentials Committee," selected years.

The executives of locals decide whether or not to send their delegates and many do not attend for a variety of reasons.

CHAPTER FOUR

1 For a more fully developed discussion see Pammett, "Class Voting and Class Consciousness in Canada," 269–90.
2 Horowitz, *Canadian Labour in Politics*, chap. 1.
3 Brodie and Jenson, *Crisis, Challenge and Change*; Laxer, *Canada's Unions*, 271–3.
4 Wood, *The Current Trade Union Scene*, 2.
5 Labour Canada, *Directory of Labour Organizations in Canada*, 1984, table E.
6 Gunderson, "Professionalization of the Canadian Public Sector," 115.
7 Olson, *The Logic of Collective Action*, chap. 1; Hardin, *Collective Action*, chap. 1.
8 The cost of union affiliation with both the British Labour party and the New Democratic party is very modest. In 1976 the fee in Britain was 20 pence per member per month. In Canada affiliation dues in 1984 averaged approximately 20 cents per member per month.
9 Both union membership and affiliation with the Labour party dropped substantially after 1920 and did not regain the pre-1920s position until after 1945. Data on the size of the labour force are from Marsh, *Trade Union Handbook*, 11–21. Data on affiliation with the Labour party are from the party's *Report of the Annual Conference*, selected years. Data on voting for the Labour party are from several sources, including Beer et al, *Patterns of Government*, 756–7; and Ranney, ed, *Britain at the Polls, 1983*, 197–9.

CHAPTER FIVE

1 See, for example, Meisel, *Working Papers on Canadian Politics*, and Clarke et al., *Political Choice in Canada*.
2 Miller, "Organized Labour and Politics in Canada," 231.
3 Chi and Perlin, "The New Democratic Party," 179.
4 Keddie, "Class Identification and Party Preference Among Manual Workers," 31.

5 See, for example, Van Loon and Whittington, *The Canadian Political System*, 141–4, and Katznelson, *City Trenches*.
6 See, among many others, Duverger, *Political Parties*, 227, Barnes, "Ideology and the Organization of Conflict," 522–30, and Sartori, "Sociology of Politics," 84–5.
7 For the importance of cues in exercising influence see Dahl, *Modern Political Analysis*, 44–53.
8 See Van Loon and Whittington, *The Canadian Political System* and Katznelson, *City Trenches*.
9 Annual reports on local union affiliation with the NDP covering the period from 1961 to 1984 were made available by the federal office of the NDP, which bears no responsibility for the analyses or interpretations presented here.
10 See, for instance, Clarke et al., *Political Choice in Canada*, 517–52.
11 Copies of the 1979 interview schedules were made available by Harold Clarke.
12 For a discussion of this grounding see Johnston, "The Geography of Class and Religion in Canadian Elections."
13 This is consistent with the aggregate proportion of union local affiliation in Canada. In 1979, 404 of the 745 affiliated locals (54 per cent) were either UAW or USWA locals, which together comprise 59 per cent of affiliated unionists. NDP files.
14 The total number of members of NDP-affiliated locals in the 1979 sample by region is: Quebec and Atlantic, 4; Ontario, 95; and the West, 30; summing to 129.
15 NDP files, 1979.

CHAPTER SIX

1 Downs, *An Economic Theory of Democracy*, chap. 3; Campbell et al, *The American Voter*, chap. 2.
2 See, for example: Jackson, "Issues, Party Choices and Presidential Voting"; Markus and Converse, "A Dynamic Simultaneous Equation Model"; Page and Jones, "Reciprocal Effects of Policy Preferences, Party Loyalties and the Vote"; and Franklin and Jackson, "The Dynamics of Party Identification."
3 Meisel, *Working Papers on Canadian Politics*, 67; Jenson, "The Filling of Wine Bottles Is Not Easy"; and Clarke et al., *Political Choice in Canada*, chap. 5.

4 LeDuc et al., "Partisan Instability in Canada," 475.
5 Page and Jones, "Reciprocal Effects of Policy Preferences, Party Loyalties and the Vote," 1077–82; Markus and Converse, "A Dynamic Simultaneous Equation Model," 1059.
6 Page and Jones, "Reciprocal Effects of Policy Preferences, Party Loyalties and the Vote," 1073. Technically, individuals vote directly for a slate of electors from their state who are part of the Electoral College and who are pledged to vote for the presidential candidate receiving a plurality of votes from their state.
7 Clarke et al., "Voting Behaviour and the Outcome of the 1979 Federal Election," 530–8.
8 Clarke et al., *Political Choice in Canada*, chap. 5.
9 Sniderman et al., "Party Loyalty and Electoral Volatility"; Jenson, "Party Loyalty in Canada"; Campbell et al., *The American Voter*. See also Johnston, "The Reproduction of the Religious Cleavage in Canadian Elections," especially 102–5.
10 Meisel, *Working Papers on Canadian Politics*, chap. 2; Clarke et al., *Political Choice in Canada*, chap. 4. An interesting explanation for the persistence of this cleavage in the electorate despite its virtual irrelevance among the parties can be found in Johnston, "The Reproduction of the Religious Cleavage in Canadian Elections," 99–113.
11 Schwartz, *Politics and Territory*; Engelmann and Schwartz, *Political Parties and the Canadian Social Structure*; and Alford, *Party and Society*. Clarke et al., *Political Choice in Canada*, 122–4. Zipp, "Social Class and Canadian Federal Electoral Behavior," chap. 3.
12 See Johnston, "The Reproduction of the Religious Cleavage in Canadian Elections," 107–12, for a discussion of the importance of political context. A classic statement of the importance of context can be found in Lazarsfeld et al., *The People's Choice*.
13 For an examination of this issue with respect to perceptions of provincial parties, see Elkins, "The Structure of Provincial Party Systems."
14 Kornberg and Archer, "A Note on Quebec Attitudes Toward Constitutional Options."
15 Fiorina, *Retrospective Voting in American National Elections*. See also Page, *Choices and Echoes in Presidential Elections*.
16 See also Kornberg et al., *Representative Democracy in the Canadian Provinces*, chap. 7.

17 Blishen and McRoberts, "A Revised Socioeconomic Index for Occupations in Canada."
18 Clarke et al., *Absent Mandate*, chap. 5.
19 Brown et al., "The 1984 Election: Explaining the Vote."
20 Johnston, "The Geography of Class and Religion in Canadian Elections"; Forbes and Sniderman, "Religion and Partisanship in Canada."

Bibliography

Alford, Robert R. *Party and Society: The Anglo-American Democracies.* Chicago: Rand-McNally 1963.
Archer, Keith. "Canadian Unions and the New Democratic Party: The Failure of Collective Action." Unpublished doctoral dissertation, Duke University, 1985.
– "Canadian Unions, the New Democratic Party, and the Problem of Collective Action." *Labour/Le Travail* 20(1987): 173–84.
– "The Failure of the New Democratic Party: Unions, Unionists and Politics in Canada." *Canadian Journal of Political Science* 18(1985): 353–66.
– "A Simultaneous Equation Model of Canadian Voting Behaviour." *Canadian Journal of Political Science* 20(1987): 553–72.
– and Alan Whitehorn. "Opinion Structure Among NDP Activists." Paper presented to the annual meeting of the Canadian Political Science Association, Windsor, Ontario, 9–11 June 1988.
Babcock, Robert H. *Gompers in Canada: A Study in American Continentalism before the First World War.* Toronto: University of Toronto Press 1974.
Barnes, Samuel H. "The Ideologies and Policies of Canadian Labor Organizations." Unpublished doctoral dissertation, Duke University, 1957.
– "Ideology and the Organization of Conflict: On the Relationship Between Political Thought and Behaviour." *Journal of Politics* 28(1966): 513–30.
Barry, Brian M. *Sociologists, Economists and Democracy.* London: Collier-Macmillan 1970.

Beer, Samuel H., Adam B. Ulam, Suzanne Berger, and Guido Goldman. *Patterns of Government: The Major Political Systems of Europe.* 3rd ed. New York: Random House 1973.

Bell, David V.J. "The Loyalist Tradition in Canada." *Journal of Canadian Studies* 5(1970): 22–33.

Berger, Suzanne, ed. *Organizing Interests in Western Europe.* Cambridge: Cambridge University Press 1981.

– and Michael J. Piore. *Dualism and Discontinuity in Industrial Societies.* Cambridge: Cambridge University Press 1980.

Blishen, Bernard R., and Hugh A. McRoberts. "A Revised Socioeconomic Index for Occupations in Canada." *Canadian Review of Sociology and Anthropology* 13(1976): 71–9.

Brodie, M. Janine, and Jane Jenson. *Crisis, Challenge and Change: Party and Class in Canada.* Toronto: Methuen 1980.

Brown, Steven, Ronald Lambert, Barry Kay, and James Curtis. "The 1984 Election: Explaining the Vote." Prepared for the annual meeting of the Canadian Political Science Association, University of Manitoba, Winnipeg, Manitoba, 6–8 June 1986.

Cairns, Alan C. "The Electoral System and the Party System in Canada, 1921–1965." *Canadian Journal of Political Science* 1(1968): 55–80.

– "The Governments and Societies of Canadian Federalism." *Canadian Journal of Political Science* 10(1977): 695–725.

Campbell, Angus, Philip E. Converse, Warren E. Miller, and Donald E. Stokes. *The American Voter.* New York: Wiley 1960.

Canada. Elections Canada. *Registered Parties Fiscal Period Returns.* Selected years.

Canada. Labour Canada. *Directory of Labour Organisations in Canada.* Selected years.

Canada. Statistics Canada. *Census.* Ottawa 1931.

Canada. Statistics Canada. *Report of the Chief Electoral Officer.* Ottawa 1974–86.

Canadian Labour 6 (September 1961): 3.

Chi, N.H. "Class Cleavage." In *Political Parties in Canada*, edited by Conrad Winn and John McMenemy. McGraw-Hill Ryerson in 1976.

– and George C. Perlin. "The New Democratic Party: A Party in Transition." In *Party Politics in Canada*, edited by Hugh G. Thorburn. 4th ed. Scarborough, Ont.: Prentice-Hall 1979.

Clarke, Harold D., Jane Jenson, Lawrence LeDuc, and Jon H. Pammett. *Absent Mandate: The Politics of Discontent in Canada.* Toronto: Gage 1984.
– *Political Choice in Canada.* Toronto: McGraw-Hill Ryerson 1979.
– "Voting Behaviour and the Outcome of the 1979 Federal Election: The Impact of Leaders and Issues." *Canadian Journal of Political Science* 15(1982): 517–52.
Dahl, Robert A. *Modern Political Analysis.* 3rd ed. Englewood Cliffs NJ: Prentice-Hall 1976.
Downs, Anthony. *An Economic Theory of Democracy.* New York: Harper and Row 1957.
Duverger, Maurice. *Political Parties.* Translated by Barbara and Robert North. London: Methuen 1964.
Elkins, David J. "The Structure of Provincial Party Systems." In *Small Worlds: Provinces and Parties in Canadian Political Life*, edited by David J. Elkins and Richard Simeon. Toronto: Metheun 1980.
Engelmann, Frederick C., and Mildred A. Schwartz. *Political Parties and the Canadian Social Structure.* Scarborough, Ont.: Prentice-Hall 1967.
Erlanger, Howard S., and Halliman H. Winsborough. "The Structure of Violence Thesis: An Example of a Simultaneous Equation Model in Sociology." *Sociological Methods and Research* 5(1976): 231–46.
Fiorina, Morris P. *Retrospective Voting in American National Elections.* New Haven CT: Yale University Press 1981.
Forbes, H.D. "Hartz-Horowitz at Twenty: Nationalism, Toryism, and Socialism in Canada and the United States." *Canadian Journal of Political Science* 20(1987): 287–315.
Forbes, H. Don, and Paul Sniderman. "Religion and Partisanship in Canada, 1965 to 1984." Prepared for the annual meeting of the Canadian Political Science Association, University of Windsor, Windsor, Ontario, 9–11 June 1988.
Forsey, Eugene. *Trade Unions in Canada, 1812–1902.* Toronto: University of Toronto Press 1982.
Franklin, Charles H., and John E. Jackson. "The Dynamics of Party Identification." *American Political Science Review* 77(1983): 957–73.
Gibbins, Roger. *Conflict and Unity: An Introduction to Canadian Political Life.* Toronto: Methuen 1985.

Gunderson, Morley. "Professionalization of the Canadian Public Sector." In *Studies in Public Employment and Compensation in Canada*, edited by Meyer W. Bucovetsky. Scarborough, Ont.: Butterworth 1979.

Hanushek, Eric A., and John E. Jackson. *Statistical Methods for Social Scientists*. New York: Academic Press 1977.

Hardin, Russell. *Collective Action*. Baltimore MD: The Johns Hopkins University Press 1982.

Hartz, Louis. *The Founding of New Societies*. New York: Harcourt, Brace & World 1964.

Horowitz, Gad. *Canadian Labour in Politics*. Toronto: University of Toronto Press 1968.

Jackson, John E. "Issues, Party Choices, and Presidential Votes." *American Journal of Political Science* 19 (1975): 161–86.

Jenson, Jane. "The Filling of Wine Bottles Is Not Easy." *Canadian Journal of Political Science* 11(1978): 437–6.

– "Party Loyalty in Canada: The Question of Party Identification." *Canadian Journal of Political Science* 8(1975): 543–53.

– "Party Strategy and Party Identification: Some Patterns of Partisan Allegiance." *Canadian Journal of Political Science* 9(1976): 27–48.

Johnston, Richard. "The Geography of Class and Religion in Canadian Elections." Prepared for the annual meeting of the Canadian Political Science Association, McMaster University, Hamilton, Ontario, 3–5 June 1987.

– "The Reproduction of the Religious Cleavage in Canadian Elections." *Canadian Journal of Political Science* 18(1985): 99–117.

Katznelson, Ira. *City Trenches: Urban Politics and the Patterning of Class in the United States*. New York: Pantheon 1981.

Keddie, Vincent. "Class Identification and Party Preference Among Manual Workers: The Influence of Community, Union Membership and Kinship." *Canadian Review of Sociology and Anthropology* 17(1980): 24–36.

Knowles, Stanley. *The New Party*. Toronto: McClelland and Stewart 1961.

Kornberg, Allan, Harold D. Clarke, and Marianne C. Stewart. "Federalism and Fragmentation: Political Support in Canada." *Journal of Politics* 41(1979): 889–905.

Kornberg, Allan, and Keith Archer. "A Note on Quebec Attitudes Toward Constitutional Options." *Law and Contemporary Problems* 43(1982): 71–85.

Kornberg, Allan, William Mishler, and Harold D. Clarke. *Representative Democracy in the Canadian Provinces*. Scarborough, Ont: Prentice-Hall 1982.

Labour Party of Great Britain. *Report of the Annual Conference*. Selected years.

Laxer, Robert. *Canada's Unions*. Toronto: Lorimer 1976.

Lazarsfeld, Paul F., Bernard Berelson, and Hazel Gaudet. *The People's Choice: How the Voter Makes Up His Mind in a Presidential Campaign*. New York: Columbia University Press 1944.

LeDuc, Lawrence. "Canada: the Politics of Stable Dealignment." In *Electoral Change in Advanced Industrial Democracies*, edited by Russell J. Dalton, Scott C. Flanagan, and Paul Allen Beck. Princeton NJ: Princeton University Press 1984.

– "Partisan Change and Dealignment in Canada, Great Britain and the United States," *Comparative Politics* 17(1985): 379–98.

– Harold D. Clarke, Jane Jenson, and Jon H. Pammett. "Partisan Instability in Canada: Evidence from a New Panel Study." *American Political Science Review* 78(1984): 470–84.

Lewis, David. *The Good Fight: Political Memoirs 1909–1958*. Toronto: Macmillan 1981.

– and Frank Scott. *Make This Your Canada: A Review of CCF History and Policy*. Toronto: Central Canada Publishing 1943.

Lipset, S.M. *Agrarian Socialism: The Cooperative Commonwealth Federation in Saskatchewan*. Rev. ed. Garden City NY: Doubleday 1968.

– *The First New Nation: The United States in Historical and Comparative Perspective*. New York: Basic Books 1963.

– and Stein Rokkan. "Introduction." In *Party Systems and Voter Alignments: Cross National Perspectives*, edited by Seymour M. Lipset and Stein Rokkan. New York: The Free Press 1967.

McDonald, Lynn. *The Party That Changed Canada: The New Democratic Party, Then and Now*. Toronto: Macmillan 1987.

McRae, K.D. "The Structure of Canadian History." In *The Founding of New Societies*, by Louis Hartz. New York: Harcourt, Brace & World 1964.

McNaught, Kenneth. *A Prophet in Politics: A Biography of J.S. Woodsworth*. Toronto: University of Toronto Press 1959.

Margolis, Michael. "From Confusion to Confusion: Issues and the American Voter (1956–1972)." *American Political Science Review* 71(1977): 31–43.

Markus, George B. "Political Attitudes During an Election Year: A Report on the 1980 NES Panel Study." *American Political Science Review* 76(1982): 538–60.

– and Philip E. Converse. "A Dynamic Simultaneous Equation Model of Electoral Choice." *American Political Science Review* 76(1982): 1055–70.

Marsh, Arthur. *Trade Union Handbook*. 2nd ed. London: Westmead 1980.

Meisel, John. *Working Papers on Canadian Politics*. 2nd ed. Montreal: McGill-Queen's University Press 1975.

Miller, Richard Ulric. "Organized Labour and Politics in Canada." In *Canadian Unions in Transition*, edited by Richard Ulric Miller and Fraser Isbester. Scarborough, Ont.: Prentice-Hall, 1971.

Minkin, Lewis. *The Labour Party Conference: A Study in the Politics of Intra Party Democracy*. London: Allen Lane 1978.

Morley, J.T. *Secular Socialists: The CCF/NDP in Ontario, A Biography*. Montreal: McGill University Press 1983.

Morton, Desmond. *NDP: The Dream of Power*. Toronto: Hakkert 1974.

– *NDP: Social Democracy in Canada*. 2nd ed. Toronto: Hakkert 1977.

– *The New Democrats 1961–1986: The Politics of Change*. Toronto: Copp Clark Pitman 1986.

– *Working People*. Rev. ed. Ottawa: Deneau 1984.

Mueller, Dennis C. *Public Choice*. Cambridge: Cambridge University Press 1979.

New Democratic Party, selected files.

Olson, Mancur, Jr. *The Logic of Collective Action: Public Goods and the Theory of Groups*. Cambridge MA: Harvard University Press 1965.

Page, Benjamin I. *Choices and Echoes in Presidential Elections: Rational Man and Electoral Democracy*. Chicago: University of Chicago Press 1978.

– and Calvin C. Jones. "Reciprocal Effects of Policy Preferences, Party Loyalties and the Vote." *American Political Science Review* 73(1979): 1071–89.

Pammett, Jon H. "Class Voting and Class Consciousness in Canada." *Canadian Review of Sociology and Anthropology* 24(1987): 269–90.

Ranney, Austin, ed. *Britain at the Polls, 1983*. Durham NC: Duke University Press 1985.

Reid, Escott. "The Rise of National Parties in Canada." In *Party Politics in Canada*. 5th ed. edited by Hugh Thorburn. Scarborough, Ont.: Prentice-Hall 1985.

Sartori, Giovanni. "From the Sociology of Politics to Political Sociology." In *Politics and the Social Sciences*, edited by Seymour Martin Lipset. New York: Oxford University Press 1969.

Schwartz, Mildred A. *Politics and Territory: The Sociology of Regional Resistance in Canada*. Montreal: McGill-Queen's University Press 1974.

Scott, Frank R. *A New Endeavour*, edited by Michiel Horn. Toronto: University of Toronto Press 1986.

Simerl, Loren M. "A Survey of Canadian Provincial Election Results, 1905–1981." In *Politics: Canada*, 5th ed., edited by Paul W. Fox. Toronto: McGraw-Hill Ryerson 1982.

Smiley, D.V. *Canada in Question: Federalism in the Eighties*. Toronto: McGraw-Hill Ryerson 1980.

Sniderman, Paul M., H.D. Forbes, and Ian Melzer. "Party Loyalty and Electoral Volatility: A Study of the Canadian Party System." *Canadian Journal of Political Science* 7(1974): 268–88.

Stanbury, W.T. "The Mother's Milk of Politics: Political Contributions to Federal Parties in Canada, 1974–1984." *Canadian Journal of Political Science* 19(1986): 795–821.

Thorburn, Hugh, ed. *Party Politics in Canada*. 4th ed. Scarborough, Ont.: Prentice-Hall 1979.

Trades Union Conference (Great Britain). *Conference Proceedings*. 1982.

Van Loon, Richard J., and Michael S. Whittington. *The Canadian Political System: Environment, Structure and Process*. 4th ed. Toronto: McGraw-Hill Ryerson 1987.

Wanner, Richard A., and Lionel S. Lewis. "The Functional Theory of Stratification: A Test of Some Structural Hypotheses." *Sociological Quarterly* 19(1978): 414–28.

Wearing, Joseph. *Strained Relations: Canada's Parties and Voters*. Toronto: McClelland and Stewart 1988.

Welch, Susan, and John C. Comer. *Quantitative Methods for Public Administration*. 2nd ed. Chicago: Dorsey 1988.

Wiseman, Nelson. *Social Democracy in Manitoba: A History of the CCF-NDP*. Winnipeg: University of Manitoba Press 1983.

Wood, W.D. *The Current Trade Union Scene: Patterns and Trends*. Kingston, Ont.: Industrial Relations Centre, Queen's University, 1976.

Young, Walter D. *The Anatomy of a Party: The National CCF 1932–1961*. Toronto: University of Toronto Press 1969.

Zakuta, Leo. *A Protest Movement Becalmed: A Study of Change in the CCF*. Toronto: University of Toronto Press 1964.

Zipp, J. "Social Class and Canadian Federal Electoral Behaviour: A Reconsideration and Elaboration." Unpublished doctoral dissertation, Duke University, 1978.

Index

ABBREVIATIONS
CCF – Co-operative Commonwealth Federation
NDP – New Democratic party

Affect, for party leaders, 78
Affiliation (union): attempts by NDP to increase, 36, 37, 38; binary choice, 44; with CCF, 12, 15; as a collective action problem, 51–4; comparison with Britain, 15, 16, 47–51; confined to Ontario under CCF, 18; and constituency control of CCF, 16; developing rules for with CCF, 15; effect on political behaviour, 56–71; explanations for failure of, 18–20, 41; and founding of NDP, 24; impact on support for NDP, 68, 69, 87–9; mobilizational capacity of, 64; as a political cue, 25, 58; problems for national organizations in, 12; rates of, 41–3; regional distribution of, 38, 39; rules of, 41; union size and, 52–4; and voting behaviour, 61–4, 71, 77

Age, effect on voting, 77
Agrarian interests: and CCF, 20; and NDP, 24
All-Canadian Congress of Labour (ACCL), 12, 13, 14
American Federation of Labor (AFL): and Committee on Industrial Organizations, 13; merger with Congress of Industrial Organizations, 21
Archer, Keith. *See* Kornberg
Atlantic region: NDP-affiliated unions in, 66, 67

Blishen, Bernard (with McRoberts), socioeconomic status index, 80
British Labour party: incentives for unions to affiliate with, 50; model for CCF and NDP, 4, 15; union affiliation with, 45–51; union representation at conferences of, 50

Broadbent, Ed, effect on voting, 79, 86–9 passim
Brodie, Janine (with Jenson): on business unionism, 41; on role of parties in highlighting political cleavages, 3n
Business unionism: impact on affiliation, 41

Campbell, Angus, approach to voting behaviour, 72, 76
Canadian and Catholic Confederation of Labour (CCCL), 13
Canadian Automobile Workers, 27. *See also* United Automobile Workers
Canadian Brotherhood of Railway Employees (CBRE), 12; and problem of affiliation of national unions to CCF, 13
Canadian Congress of Labour (CCL): creation, 14; merger with Trades and Labor Congress, 21; ties with CCF, 14

Index

Canadian Federation of Labour, 13

Canadian Labour Congress (CLC): and affiliation of unions, 51–2; creation, 21; personnel links to NDP, 27, 36; Political Education Committee, 21, 30; role in formation of NDP, 4, 23

Canadian Labour party, 11

Candidate evaluation: importance in American political behaviour, 75; influence of affiliation status on, 68, 69; role in Canadian voting behaviour, 73, 74

Chi, N.H. (with Perlin), on impact of union membership on vote, 56

Clark, Joe, effect on voting, 76, 79, 80, 81, 84–6

Clarke, Harold, on predictors of voting behaviour, 76, 77

Class: and affiliation with NDP, 6; effect on voting, 79; self-images and union status, 69, 70

Coldwell, M.J., 23

Collective action problems, and union-party affiliation, 41–55 passim

Committee on Industrial Organizations, 13

Communists, and affiliation with CCF, 18

Community size, effect on voting, 77

Congress of Industrial Organizations (CIO): creation, 13, 14; merger with American Federation of Labor, 21

Constituency strength, as a predictor of NDP voting, 65, 66, 67

Converse, Philip. *See* Markus

Co-operative Commonwealth Federation (CCF): and British Labour party model, 15; decline after 1945, 19–20; and development of NDP, 5, 22–5, 27; electoral performance at provincial level 1944–60, 17, 20; electoral success 1941–4, 16, 17; emergence of, 8–13; as political arm of labour, 18

Crerar, T.A., 10

Determinants of voting, in reciprocal model, 79–80

Diefenbaker, John, 23

Direction of voting, predictors of, 78

Dominion Labour party (Alberta), 11

Downs, Anthony, model of voting behaviour, 72

Education, effect on voting, 77

Elections: Ontario provincial, 17, 19; studies of Canadian, 56, 59, 80–1

Engelmann, Frederick (with Schwartz), and contextual variables in voting behaviour, 77

Farmers: coalition with labour, 11; and NDP, 24; political influence of, 10

Federal Council (NDP): membership and role in party, 29

Fiorina, Morris, on voting behaviour, 78

Free rider issue, in collective action problems, 41, 45, 49, 55

Gardiner, Robert, 10

Garland, E.J., 10

Gompers, Samuel: approach to political action, 12; application of approach in Canadian context, 21

Government performance, effect on voting, 78

Gunderson, Morley, on public sector unions, 43–4

Hartz, Louis, and fragment thesis, 41

Heaps, A.A., 11

Horowitz, Gad: explanations for CCF weaknesses, 18–20; on failure of affiliation movement, 41; on similarities of CCF and NDP, 25; on Trades and Labor Congress policy on political action, 21

Ideological self-placement, and union status, 69–70

Incentives, 45; for union affiliation with British Labour party, 50; for union affiliation with the NDP, 52–3

Independent Labour party, 9, 11

Industrial unions, emergence of, 13, 14

International Brotherhood of Electrical Workers (IBEW), 18

International Woodworkers of America (IWA), 18

Irvine, William, 9, 10

Issues (election): effect of assessment on voting, 73, 74; positions on as predictors of voting, 77, 78

Index

Jenson, Jane. *See* Brodie
Jones, Calvin C. *See* Page

Keddie, V., on link between union membership and vote, 57
Knowles, Stanley, 11; and emergence of NDP, 23–4
Kornberg, Allan, 80; (with Archer) on sociodemographic determinants of attitudes, 77, 78

Labour: agenda in NDP, 29; and creation of NDP, 27; domination of CCF/NDP prevented, 28; early coalition with farmers, 11; early links to political parties, 7, 8; financial links to NDP, 33–5; personnel links to NDP, 27–31; representation at NDP conventions, 28, 54; representation on NDP Federal Council, 29
Leader evaluation: effect on voting, 81–9; predictors of, 78, 79
League for Social Reconstruction (LSR), 11; and creation of CCF, 11
LeDuc, Lawrence, on party partisanship, 73
Lewis, David, 28; on labour ties with CCF, 14, 15; personal links with labour leaders, 14; on replacement of CCF with NDP, 25; on rules of union affiliation, 15–18, 23–5, 95n; on Trades and Labor Congress expulsion of Congress of Industrial Organizations unions, 14
Liberal party: determinants of voting for, 81–4; effect of union affiliation on votes for, 61–3; financing, 35, 39; history, 9, 10; support among NDP-affiliated unionists, 64
Liberalism, 5; and failure of affiliation movement, 41

MacInnis, Angus, 11; and union affiliation with CCF, 15
MacPhail, Agnes, 10
McRoberts, Kenneth. *See* Blishen
Markus, Gregory (with Converse), model of voting behaviour, 75, 76
Maximum utility decision rule, 5, 41–55 *passim*
Miller, Richard U., on union voting patterns, 56
Mine Mill Workers, 18
Morton, Desmond: on impact of communists on affiliation, 18; on labour at NDP founding convention, 30; on labour domination in NDP, 25
Mosher, A.R., 12, 13

National Committee for a New Party (NCNP), 23, 28
New Democratic party (NDP): challenge to labour's role, 28; changing image of, 27; composition and role of Federal Council, 29; constitution, 28; determinants of voting for, 79, 86–9; effect of union affiliation on voting, 61–3; electoral weakness of, 3–5; financial contributions to, 31–5; founding of, 23–4, 30–2; personnel links between unions and, 27–31; representation at conventions of, 28, 54; similarities with CCF, 24; stability of vote for, 64; and union affiliation, 35–9; voting for among union members, 56–7, 87–9
Noseworthy, J.W., 16, 17

One Big Union, 13
Ontario: elections, 17, 19; unions affiliated with NDP in, 66, 67

Page, Benjamin (with Jones), model of voting behaviour, 75, 76
Pammett, Jon, 98n
Party identification: consistency, 76, 79; effect of union affiliation on, 62–3; flexibility of in Canada, 72, 73; intergenerational transfer of, 76; strength of, 79
Party images, and affiliation status, 68–9
Pawley, Howard, on fears of union domination, 24
Perlin, George. *See* Chi
Personnel links, between labour and NDP, 27–31
Political Education Committee (Canadian Labour Congress), 21, 30
Prairie provinces: rise of third parties in, 8, 9, 10, 11; unions affiliated with NDP in, 66, 67
Progressive Conservative party: determinants of voting for, 79, 84–6; early history, 8, 9, 10; effect of union affiliation on voting for, 61–3; financing of, 35, 39;

support among NDP-affiliated unionists, 64-6
Progressive party, 9-10
Protestants, traditional voting patterns, 76
Public choice approach to political behaviour, 5, 55
Public sector unions, 42-4

Quebec, unions affiliated with NDP in, 66, 67

Rational choice model, applied to affiliation decision, 44-6, 49
Reciprocal model of voting behaviour: described, 73-80; applied to Liberal vote, 81-4; applied to NDP vote, 86-9; applied to Progressive Conservative vote, 84-6
Regina Manifesto (1933), 11
Region, and voting patterns, 66-7, 77
Religion, impact on voting, 76, 79-80
Retrospective voting, 71
Roman Catholics, traditional voting patterns, 76

Saskatchewan, election of 1944, 17
Schwartz, Mildred, and contextual variables in voting behaviour, 77
Social cleavages: electoral importance of, 64; and politicization, 64
Socialism, 12
Socialist party, 11; of British Columbia, 11
Socialization, 57; adult, 59; importance of family, 59, 76

Socio-economic status, effect on voting, 77
Spencer, Henry, 10

Third parties, rise of, 8-13
Trades and Labor Congress (TLC): and Berlin conference, 13; expulsion of Congress of Industrial Organizations unions, 14; Gomperist approach to politics, 12; merger with Canadian Congress of Labour, 21; policy towards political action, 21
Trades Union Congress (TUC), links with British Labour party, 15, 46-51
Trudeau, Pierre Elliott, effect on voting, 79-84

Underhill, Frank, 11; and Regina Manifesto, 11
Union affiliation: as a behavioural cue, 6; as a decision rule, 5; effect on union members, 4, 61-71; effect on voting, 61-3, 81-9; individual and aggregate effects, 5
Union movement: changes in 1921-40, 13; growth, 1966-84, 42-3
Unions: American based, 41; effect on vote of membership in, 56-7; financial links to NDP, 31-5; national versus international, 43; personnel links with NDP, 27-31; public sector, 42-4
Unions, NDP-affiliated: effect of membership on attitudes and behaviour, 60-71; members in sample, 61; operationalization of membership in, 60-1

United Automobile Workers (UAW), 18; and union affiliation, 64; voting patterns of, 65
United Mine Workers, District 26, affiliates with CCF, 15
United Steelworkers of America (USWA): and union affiliation, 64; voting patterns, 65
Utility maximization, 41, 54; as a decision rule, 5

Volatility, of electorate, 64
Voting behaviour: American models of, 75, 76; effect of union membership on, 56, 57; estimations of, 3-4; impact of short- and long-term factors in, 72, 90; importance of attitudinal variables, 89; prediction of, 72, 73, 78; reciprocal model of, 74-9; and union affiliation, 62, 63

West: unions affiliated with NDP in, 66, 67
Western Labour Conference, 11
Winnipeg Declaration of Principles (1956), 22
Wiseman, Nelson: on similarities of CCF and NDP, 24; on similarities of CCF and NDP convention delegates, 29; on union affiliation, 25; on union affiliation with the CCF, 35
Woodsworth, J.S., 9, 10, 11

York South by-election (1942), 16, 17

Zipp, John: on effect of party constituency strength on voting, 77